Praise for the book
Because We Care:
A Handbook for Chaplaincy in
Emergency Medical Services

Research shows that people who work as EMTs, paramedics, and dispatchers experience more stress, anxiety,
depression, and PTSD than the general population. A
clinically trained chaplain can become a vital part of the
support system for these professionals who spend their
lives running toward danger rather than away from it.

In this book, Russ Myers does a masterful job of
weaving together modern leadership perspectives, evidence-based psychological concepts, spiritual support,
and deep compassion for the folks who spend their lives
helping others through medical emergencies. Experienced or aspiring chaplains and EMS leaders will benefit
from Russ's perspective.

Mike Taigman
Former paramedic, resilience expert,
and law enforcement/EMS educator
Author, Super-Charge Your Stress Management
in the Age of Covid-19: A Handbook for Emergency
Services and Healthcare Professionals

A thoughtful and practical re
workplace chaplaincy in any

and the organizational leaders who employ them will benefit from the wisdom and insight Russ shares. This book is a valuable contribution to the professional chaplaincy literature. The examples and reflections that Russ provides take you to the heart of what it means to show up, care deeply, and engage fully during crisis.

Karen Hutt
ACPE educator
VP for Student Formation, Vocation, and Innovation
United Theological Seminary of the Twin Cities
Editor, The Call to Care: Essays by Unitarian Universalist Chaplains

As Russell Myers observes, chaplaincy has changed much over the last few decades, and this book is a timely reminder that chaplaincy is a specialized ministry requiring its own set of skills. He argues well for professionalism but not losing the aims and unique ministry of being alongside people. He gives plenty of food for thought and practical suggestions.

Revd. Dr. Fiona Stewart-Darling
Lead Chaplain, Multifaith Chaplaincy Team
Supporting Organizations and their Employees
in Financial Centre of Canary Wharf, London, UK
Author, Multifaith Chaplaincy in the Workplace

BECAUSE WE CARE

A HANDBOOK FOR CHAPLAINCY IN EMERGENCY MEDICAL SERVICES

BY

RUSSELL N. MYERS

GRYPHON'S KEY
PUBLISHING

An Imprint of Progressive Rising Phoenix Press

Published 2021 by
Gryphon's Key Publishing
An Imprint of Progressive Rising Phoenix Press, LLC
www.gryphonskeypublishing.com

ISBN: 978-1-950560-54-7

Printed in the U.S.A.

Editor: Jody Amato

Cover Photo: "Team of EMS Paramedics Provide Help to an Injured Young Man. Doctor in Gloves Attaches Cervical Neck Collar on a Patient. Emergency Care Assistants Arrived in an Ambulance Vehicle at Night" Royalty-free stock photo ID: 1878018178 By Gorodenkoff. Image used under license from Shutterstock.com.

Cartoon reprinted by permission. © King Features Syndicate, Inc. World rights reserved.
https://comicskingdom.com/safe-havens

Umbrella Clipart from onlinewebfonts.com/icon is licensed by CC 3.0.

Toleration of Pain Chart: Source: "Leadership in Healthy Congregations," https://www.healthycongregations.com

Book cover and interior design by William Speir
Visit: http://www.williamspeir.com

Organizing these thoughts and sharing my work with peers and colleagues has been a privilege.

To my family and friends: hopefully this will explain what I do every day, and why it matters. Thank you for your support.

I wrote almost all of it
in the deepest hope and conviction.
Sifting my thoughts
and choosing my words.
Trying to say what was true.
And I'll tell you frankly,
that was wonderful.

from *Gilead*
by Marilynne Robinson

Table of Contents

Foreword

It was 2006 and I sat in a routine meeting within my healthcare system, among fifteen or so hospital presidents and specialty operation leaders, including Emergency Medical Services (EMS).

Reverend Russ Myers had fifteen minutes on the agenda to speak about how he thought spiritual care at our hospital system could be enriched. He spoke about a vision that enhanced human interaction and searched for ideas from the group about how to further reach and support our staff members.

As I went home and fell asleep that night, I could not shake his comments from my mind. I had recent and raw images of people like Father Mychal Fallon Judge, the FDNY chaplain being carried away from the Twin Towers after being killed in the 9/11 attacks. I knew from personal experience the emotional drain associated with being an EMT, paramedic, or dispatcher, and I had a sense that perhaps Russ could help us, as an organization, support our employees.

Russ took this opportunity and ran with it. He literally has spent years cultivating relationships with

EMS providers and bringing lifesaving support to life-savers on the front lines.

He has created the road map for EMS agencies to leverage the role of EMS chaplain to create a supportive environment within which staff can thrive, and he also offers the business case for leaders to get behind these efforts. Agencies that show compassion and support for employees enhance recruitment and retention opportunities and separate themselves from the pack.

At a time when our nation is experiencing a paramedic shortage, COVID-related issues, and generally tough times, this book provides guidance and a business case to support the role of the EMS chaplain.

Enjoy.

Brian LaCroix
National Registered Paramedic (retired)
Fellow, American College of Paramedic Executives
President/EMS Chief (retired), Allina Health EMS

Preface

To narrate this book demands a set of perspectives that have evolved over the past thirty years. In my professional life I am a Lutheran pastor; a clinically trained, board-certified chaplain; adjunct seminary faculty member; a colleague and mentor; and the spouse of a chaplain. The sum of my experiences, and the awareness that we are charting a course for the future, have led me to write the words that follow. My process, when reading others' work, is to pay attention to the footnotes and explore the authors' sources. It has led to some fascinating discoveries and connections. I encourage you to follow the footnotes and references, wherever they lead you.[1]

The goals of this book are to articulate the role and purpose of the EMS chaplain, to provide both a business case and a human case for EMS chaplaincy, and to gently push the skeptic to reconsider the position of professional chaplain and its place in the organization. If I were to describe a physical audience for a discussion of the topics included here, the front rows would be filled with leaders of EMS agencies that have a chaplain, and those who are exploring ways to enhance their support of the frontline staff. Next in the audience are leaders doing their due diligence for hiring a workplace chaplain. Farther back and filling in the aisle seats is the community of chaplains—peers, colleagues, and students, some of whom are considering EMS or workplace chaplaincy as a vocation. Combined, it is for the reader who is curious about how the worlds of professional chaplaincy and emergency medical services intersect.

A risk for any writer is to elicit a response of tl; dr (too long; didn't read). Your level of interest in various sections of the book may vary, depending on which row of the audience you occupy. Permission is granted to skim over, skip ahead, bookmark, and return to the sections that speak to you most clearly. Theory and practice get intertwined here, with discussion of both how to think about EMS chaplaincy and how to do it.

Chapter One provides an introduction to the field of chaplaincy. The section "What Is Chaplaincy?" will offer the EMS leader an overview and reflection on current issues in chaplaincy.

Chapters Two, Three, and Four utilize the work of author and motivational speaker Simon Sinek as a framework.[2] In his 2009 book, *Start with Why*, Sinek describes several well-known companies and movements that had two people in leadership positions, one who had the vision (the "why" person) and one who was able to bring that cause to life (the "how" person). Some examples are Bill Gates and Paul Allen at Microsoft, Steve Jobs and Steve Wozniak at Apple, and Martin Luther King, Jr. and Ralph Abernathy in the civil rights movement. One person has a vision of the "why" and enlists the support of someone else with the "how" skill set to put flesh on the bones of the vision. In the Foreword, Brian LaCroix tells the story of how we met in 2006. When he asked me to serve as EMS chaplain, I demurred. I told him I already had a job but would be glad to help him find someone. He spoke about his vision for the role, which would be focused on caring for the caregivers. Brian was the "why" person at Allina Health EMS, and I became the "how." Following Sinek's model, I will start in Chapter Two with "why," then proceed to "how" in Chapter Three, before getting to the "what" in Chapter Four.

Why *(Statement of belief)*
- EMS is a high-stress job. Our employees have a right to be supported.
- We care about our employees' emotional, mental, physical, and spiritual well-being.

How *(Values or principles that guide how you bring your cause to life).* The guiding values and principles for EMS chaplaincy fall into two categories:

- Theological
- Professional

What (*Strategy, consistent with **How***)
- Proactively build relationships
- Reactively, in response to request and referrals
- Support an organizational culture of "High Expectations, High Support"
  o Collaborate with leaders in providing support to employees
  o Provide resources for self-care and stress management

I used to think that "why" the position of EMS chaplain exists is for staff support. I now recognize that staff support is part of the "what." Why EMS chaplaincy? Because we care.

Russell N. Myers
January 1, 2021

Introduction
Terra Incognita

Terra incognita (Latin for "unknown land") is a term used in cartography for regions that have not been mapped or documented. Until now, EMS chaplaincy has been a *terra incognita*. This book comes after fourteen years of exploration, discovery, and trial and error at mapping this unknown territory.

In our and other EMS organizations, field supervisors drive an SUV or squad car, making the rounds of ambulance bases and assisting crews with calls. One spring day, I was riding with a supervisor in a rural area. A call came over the radio for a patient who had fallen at home, with unknown injuries. We were in the area, so the supervisor radioed in that we would be responding to assist.

The property address was on a well-marked county road, house number 8550. As we neared the address, it became apparent that the road was the dividing line between two townships. The houses on the north side of the street were four-digit numbers in the

4000s; those on the south side were in the 8000s. Heading west, the numbers on the south side of the road were getting smaller, indicating that we had already passed the property. In fact, the GPS showed the home to be on the corner of an intersection about a half mile behind us. However, there were no structures at that intersection and no property numbers.

The county sheriff came toward us, heading east, responding to the same call. Stopping to compare notes, the sheriff said he hadn't seen a post for 8550, and since the numbers were getting bigger going east, he would continue in that direction. We continued west, and after about one-hundred yards saw a mailbox next to a dirt driveway, with the number 8550. A barn was set back from the road. We pulled in, approached the barn, and saw the house about two-hundred feet across the yard, only to realize that there was no driveway connecting the barn to the house.

Being spring in the upper Midwest, the ground was soft, and we did not want to get stuck. Mud flew as we turned around in the driveway. The supervisor drove back out onto the county road and continued west to the next driveway, leading to the house. By then we could see that the ambulance was already there and the crew was inside, tending to the patient. The sheriff soon followed us in.

This rural area was not a *terra incognita*. It was on the map. Yet our experience showed us that sometimes the map is incomplete, or the territory has changed since the map was drawn.

In the case of EMS chaplaincy, what few maps I have found have been incomplete, created to meet other needs, or based on a nonclinical chaplaincy model. The most common may be a traditional model of public safety chaplaincy, which largely draws its members from community clergy who are trained to serve in a specific context. By design, those positions tend to be reactive in nature, in which the chaplain responds when requested. The service they provide is valuable to the agencies and communities being served and gives an example of what emergency services chaplaincy might look like. They meet a vital need and are respected for their commitment to supporting the public safety workforce.

In terms of providing support to personnel, a look at the map shows Emergency Medical Services standing at a busy intersection, with several options for where to go next. Two are well-marked paths; a third is still being mapped. The well-marked paths include volunteer EMS services and some paid services, which will likely follow the on-call chaplain model. A second possible route is to forego chaplaincy and utilize support services provided by EMS leadership, mental health, EAP, and other contracted services.

The focus of this book is to proceed past the intersection, following a map that is still being drawn, exploring EMS as an emerging venue for professional chaplaincy. Setting off into the unmapped *terra incognita* of the professional EMS chaplain requires a new paradigm. This is a proactive model in which the chaplain is employed and initiates contact with and support of EMS personnel. The pages that follow are an effort to draw the map, to share my learnings with both present and future EMS leaders and chaplains.

Chapter One
Welcome to EMS Chaplaincy

Ooching into EMS Chaplaincy

After four-and-a-half years in congregational ministry and a yearlong Clinical Pastoral Education[*][3] residency at a Level 1 trauma hospital, I was hired as chaplain at United Hospital in St. Paul, Minnesota. Thirteen years later, I got the call from Brian LaCroix. I was familiar with the emotional weight of caring for people in crisis, and thought I was prepared.

Looking back now, I realize that I probably knew about as much then as the general public. Which is to say, not much. I was new to EMS, and assumed that most calls were trauma calls, and that my work would revolve around critical incident stress and debriefing. I thought it was mostly lights and sirens, high drama, and high stress on a daily basis. Now I

---

[*]Clinical Pastoral Education (CPE) is the primary method of training chaplains and spiritual care providers. More information is provided in endnote 3.

know that yes, there are lights and sirens, but trauma calls make up a small percentage of the total.

It also became clear to me that some of the people I was there to support were unclear as to my identity and role as EMS chaplain. It would take some time for us to get to know each other. As Lisa Clouzet wrote in "Chaplaincy: Are You called?":

> *A few years ago, a board-certified chaplain randomly interviewed people in New York City's Bryant Park to find out what the word* chaplain *meant to them. Many simply responded, "A what?" or repeated the question, "What is a chaplain?" back to the interviewer before admitting that they had no idea. Some of those interviewed associated the word chaplain with the military, religion, Catholics, books, and even Charlie Chaplin! A few seemed quite confident in their answers of "a preacher"; "a member of the clergy"; "someone who works in the church"; and "a pastor who serves in the hospital, police department, or fire department." Except for a woman who stated she was a former chaplain, the majority of adults questioned seemed unsure of their responses.[4]*

A physician colleague recounts a visit to a bear

sanctuary in Alaska. A ranger there told her that the way a bear will react to you is directly related to its previous experience with other humans. He said he would be terrified to walk in the wild in Glacier National Park, where the bears had people taunt, feed, and put pressure on them. At the sanctuary, the rangers were granted right of way, admired from a distance, slept outdoors, and cooked in a cooking cabin.[5]

Upon first meeting, chaplains often have a similar experience—the way people react to the chaplain is related to the person's own personal history. Positive, indifferent, or negative responses are informed by their previous experience. The experienced chaplain has learned not to take any of those personally.

Stopping at a gas station to fill up one day after work, I was wearing my jacket with "Chaplain" emblazoned across the lapel. The man behind the counter smiled and said hello. After exchanging some small talk, he nodded at my jacket and asked, "Is that the name of the company you work for?" He had no idea who or what a chaplain was.

***

My EMS position required just one day a week, and I continued to work at the hospital four days a week. I rode with ambulance crews and sat with dispatchers and went to events where I could connect with other employees. I enjoyed learning about a new venue for chaplaincy, though my primary self-identity was as a hospital chaplain with an interesting side job.

A year into the position, I noticed that while EMS involves trauma and critical incidents, it appeared also to include cumulative stress—the chronic, low-level, day in/day out work of caring for people in need. It wasn't enough for me to function in reactive mode. There was potential to expand and transform the role of EMS chaplain from reactive to proactive.

The business strategy that Brian used is called "ooch." To ooch is to construct small experiments to test one's hypothesis.[6] Rather than jump headfirst, the ooch allows the user to dip a toe in before committing to more. In this case, hire a chaplain on a limited basis, see if it's a good fit, and test the concept. I didn't have the vocabulary for it at the time, but I was ooching as well. I kept my familiar job at the hospital while I tested the waters at EMS. After a year, we both were ready for more. My hospital job decreased and the EMS responsibilities ooched up to a half-time position.

At that point, I knew I needed to learn more about EMS as an industry. This is workplace chaplaincy.[*7] In her book *Multifaith Chaplaincy in the*

---

*Unlike institutional chaplaincy, found in healthcare, corrections, military, education, and other institutions, workplace

Workplace, Chaplain Fiona Stewart-Darling highlights the importance of understanding the local and wider context and environment in which the chaplaincy will operate. Chaplains work on someone else's territory, and so: "In order to develop a chaplaincy that is able to function and deliver relevant activities, we need to understand the world in which the chaplaincy will operate, the challenges and issues that people and businesses face. Chaplains will also need to be aware of the boundaries in which they operate, and adhere to them, as well as respecting the culture and working environments.[8]"

Stewart-Darling writes of recognizing that, in her chaplaincy position in a financial center, "It was important to at least have a fundamental working knowledge of economics."[9] Likewise, it was important for me to increase my understanding of the world of the ambulance service. I enrolled in an Emergency Medical Technician (EMT) course, with a goal of learning more about the work that my coworkers do. Auditing the class, I didn't want to *be* an EMT, but rather to get a better understanding of the field of emergency medical services. In addition to the course content, I gained a deep appreciation and respect for EMTs and paramedics, who remain calm in difficult

---

chaplaincy is located in business and industry, with a focus on employees. See also endnote 7.

situations while providing emergency care. I scored fairly well on the tests but discovered my own limits when faced with the skills portion of the class. I could feel my anxiety rising when I was challenged to respond to the scenarios.

The position remained part-time for eight years and has since grown into a full-time job no longer paired with the hospital. At the time of this writing, the position is shared among three chaplains. We recognize that the concepts and practices of psychological first aid[10] and critical incident debriefing[11] and follow-up remain vital yet are secondary to a broader approach and need for ongoing and long-term emotional and spiritual health that instills resilience. Debriefings and one-to-one support remain in the toolbox, along with the work of creating and nurturing a culture of support. Chaplains are one way to provide a means for addressing well-being without giving the message that there is something wrong with you if you struggle to cope with the stress of your job. Stress is a normal response to an abnormal event. The focus is on long-term well-being and not just incidents.

This approach is not unique to EMS. Healthcare in the U.S. is being transformed to focus on preventative care. Businesses of every size encourage employees to eat healthy, exercise, get enough sleep, and tend to their spirituality. It is in the organization's best interests to provide support and resources for employee well-being. Rather than being seen as an expense, employee support is viewed as an investment. The costs of employee turnover are well documented.[12] These services are provided by a variety of practitioners; I believe chaplains are one of those, and uniquely positioned to serve in Emergency Medical Services.

What Is Chaplaincy?
What Is Professional Chaplaincy?

The word *chaplain* comes from the early history of the Christian church.

> *Traditionally, a story relates the compassion of a fourth-century holy man named Martin, who shared his cloak with a beggar. Upon the death of Bishop Martin, his cloak (*capella *in Latin) was enshrined as a reminder of the sacred act of compassion. The guardian of the capella became known as the chapelain, which, transliterated into English, became chaplain. Today the chaplain continues to guard the sacred and to share his or her cape out of compassion.[13]*

With its roots in religious tradition, modern chaplaincy focuses on providing care and compassion in secular settings. Chaplains are found in a wide variety of venues and come with a range of education and training. Many are clergy; others come into chaplaincy from the fields of counseling, teaching, social work, or psychology.

No Common Definition or Standards

Today we take standardization for granted, but it hasn't always been that way. As Daniel Immerwahr notes in *How to Hide an Empire: a History of the Greater United States*:

> *In 1904, a massive fire ravaged Baltimore. Engine companies sped from New York, Philadelphia, Annapolis, Wilmington, and Harrisburg to help. Yet there was little they could do, for when they arrived, they found that their hoses couldn't connect to Baltimore's hydrants (or, indeed, to one another's hoses). For thirty helpless hours, they watched as 1,562 buildings burned.[14]*

Imagine the scene of a major incident, with requests for mutual aid. The National Registry of Emergency Medical Technicians (NREMT)[15] does not exist; every ambulance service trains and certifies its paramedics to its own standards. Ambulances from different services arrive only to find that they are limited in their ability to assist each other, because each has had different training and uses different equipment. We shudder at the thought. Yet that is precisely the situation in which EMS chaplaincy finds itself. A Google search will bring up many certifying organizations, but there is no single standard for chaplains, and no national registry for EMS chaplains.

***

The Critical Incident Stress Management (CISM)[16] team in our area is a volunteer organization with members from law enforcement, fire, EMS, mental health, and chaplaincy. Some years ago, the team leadership received applications for membership from individuals who identified themselves as chaplains. The CISM leaders themselves came from fields that have clear professional standards and recognized that they were not seeing a common credential for chaplains. They approached the chaplains on the team with a request to set a standard definition of who could serve on the team as a chaplain. They proposed using ordination[17] as a credential.

However, there is no common process across all religions and faith communities for identifying and recognizing leaders. Some Christian denominations ordain after a minister has completed graduate theological education; others ordain prior to the start of a candidate's formal education and training. Some religious traditions do not ordain leaders. It was obvious that without common use of the concept of ordination and lacking a universal definition among the religious traditions that do use the term, *ordination* would not suffice as a criterion for chaplains. A different set of standards had to be developed for vetting the capacity of the applicants to serve as chaplains on the CISM team.

This is the same issue facing EMS agencies and any other organization seeking to utilize the services of a chaplain. We are not yet at a place in history where there is a common definition of chaplain. Each employer sets its own standard. The leaders of each organization have to decide the scope of practice, expectations, and boundaries they have in mind for their chaplain. What are the needs? What are the goals? What education, training, and credentials constitute a reasonable hiring standard? In the following pages, I will describe some of the relevant history and issues related to chaplaincy to assist EMS leaders and HR staff in making an informed decision. In the end, each employing organization has to decide what kind of chaplain it wants, and each chaplain has to decide what kind of chaplain they want to be.

In recent decades, professional disciplines such as law, education, and healthcare have increased the requirements for education, training, and certification. Some of the changes are related to specializations. Two examples are teachers and physicians. One might see specialization as preschool teachers, high school teachers, teachers of art, music, sports, and languages. It is the same in medicine. Clouzet writes:

> *In the healthcare setting, pediatricians (insert specialty of your choice) are physicians. They have studied and completed the requirements to become a physician. But pediatricians are also specialists within the wider field of medicine. Their specialty defines what type of medicine they concentrate on. Pediatricians (or orthopedists, cardiac surgeons, etc.) are to medicine what chaplains are to ministry: specialists within their field.*
>
> *Just as "physician" is a general term, so is "minister" (or "pastor"). And just as there are many specialists within the field of medicine, so many specialists also exist within the area of ministry. Youth pastor is a specialty; "chaplain" also designates a specialty of ministry.*
>
> *Chaplains have training and skills that congregational pastors usually do not have. Areas of chaplaincy can similarly be broken down according to where the chaplain ministers. For*

example, we would refer to clergy who serve in the military as military chaplains, those working in prisons as prison chaplains, and so on.[18]

Chaplaincy is undergoing a transition toward increased professionalism with standardized credentials, accountabilities, and specializations. One can barely say "teacher," "doctor," or "chaplain" without clarifying what kind of teacher, doctor, or chaplain. Where do they work? What is their specialty?

Cobb, Swift, and Todd define chaplaincy as *"a practice of care involving the intentional recognition and articulation of the sacred by nominated individuals authorized for this task in secular situations."*[19] The title "chaplain" today is a generic term used to describe these "nominated individuals." And, by definition, chaplaincy is located in secular situations. It is a profession that operates at the intersection of the sacred and the nonreligious. This understanding of secularity "goes beyond simple neutrality and implies both a freedom of conscience to hold different beliefs and a mutual respect and equality between people regardless of their sacred orientations."[20]

Chaplaincy is a practical and a relational discipline—relational in the sense that it depends on the chaplain's ability to understand and/or identify the needs of those being cared for, and the chaplain's acceptance of responsibility for meeting some or all of those needs. While many professional groups provide care to individuals and organizations, the distinctiveness of chaplaincy is in its attention to the sacred. The term *sacred* includes but is not limited to religious traditions and practices; the sacred can be expressed in all aspects of human thought and behavior, including beliefs, values, objects, and places.[21]

Traditional and Professional Chaplains

Sociologist Wendy Cadge, in writing about hospital chaplaincy departments, uses the terms *traditional* and *professional*.[22] These terms will be applied to individual chaplains here, using the definitions below. The key distinctions are in education and training, and the chaplain's boundaries and orientation to a code of ethics. These distinctions are intended only as a descriptor, which I offer here for the purpose of introducing chaplaincy to those unfamiliar with the field. Chaplains in both groups provide skilled and compassionate care.

Clinically trained professional chaplains have completed the education and training required for board certification and adhere to a code of ethics prohibiting proselytizing. Some have taken the additional step of completing the certification process and are *board-certified professional chaplains.*

For purposes of our discussion, I describe *traditional chaplains* as including those who may have completed the education and training for certification but are not held to the same boundaries around religion, and/or chaplains who have not completed all of the graduate education and clinical training requirements for certification.

Traditional

Among the ranks of chaplains are congregational clergy who make a lateral move into chaplaincy. Some find employment as chaplains in healthcare and faith-friendly businesses. With an orientation to the institutional setting, experienced clergy possessing good interpersonal and pastoral care skills provide very effective chaplaincy services.

The requirements to serve as a public safety chaplain vary by institution. The qualifications are determined by the chief or leader designated to provide oversight of the chaplain corps. Those who are clergy come with the theological education required by their religious tradition and may receive practical training in their local community. A valuable resource is the Crisis, Trauma, and First Response Certificate, offered by the Spiritual Care Association.[23] While I will advocate for professional chaplaincy, I recognize that many ambulance services will not have access to clinically trained chaplains. Whatever model the agency chooses, I emphasize the importance of having a code of ethics built into the program, for the protection of everyone.

Professional Chaplains and Credentialing

Cadge's account of "professional" hospital chaplaincy departments is also descriptive of the professional model of EMS chaplaincy that I advocate. The use of the word *professional* refers not to whether the chaplain is paid, though I do advocate for salary on par with chaplains in other contexts, such as healthcare or military. Here the term is used to denote specialized clinical training and adherence to a code of ethics.

Many public safety chaplains are eligible or working toward board certification. The distinction brought by credentialing is the acknowledgement by other disciplines that the chaplain is held to the same high standards as everyone else. No EMS agency would hire a physician who was not qualified to serve as medical director. Nor would they hire EMTs or paramedics who had not met the standards for their profession. It is in the hiring organization's—as well as in the chaplain's—best interests for the chaplain to demonstrate their accountability by earning an appropriate, recognized credential.

Professional chaplains will have an undergraduate degree, a graduate degree (usually in theology or a related field), clinical training and experience, and are eligible to be certified by a professional chaplaincy organization relevant to their field.[24] It is important to note that not all chaplains are clergy, nor are all chaplains affiliated with a religious tradition. Recent decades have seen the entrance of many highly qualified people into the field of professional chaplaincy who do not come from the historical roots of ordained clergy. The ranks of professional chaplains include secular chaplains, as well as people from a wide variety of religious and nonreligious backgrounds.

In this model, the chaplain is treated as a professional who makes a distinct contribution to the team, with measurable outcomes. The professional chaplaincy report structure leads to a director, or other senior leader, and is accountable to the institution.

Besides being an issue of integrity for the individual chaplain, the employing organization has a business interest in encouraging all of their employees to be credentialed in their respective fields. Adhering to an externally validated professional standard protects the organization, and everyone affiliated with it, by reducing the risk of malpractice. Clear and publicly stated standards of practice and behavior provide a layer of quality assurance. Rather than being a burden, professional standards, annual goals and reviews, and meeting expectations for performance are an asset and should be common practice for chaplains, as they are for everyone else. These business practices demonstrate that the organization recognizes the professional nature of the position.

Traditional chaplains who are paid by or strongly identified with a particular faith community are faced with the same expectations as professional chaplains, in that they must work with a broad and inclusive understanding of the spiritual.[25] Theology educator Alan Billings notes that chaplains working in public institutions are required to accept that "modern chaplaincy is different from how chaplaincy would be if they alone were sponsoring it or if they were only ministering to their own members."[26]

Modern Chaplaincy

Chaplaincy emerged as a profession in the twentieth century, and over the past fifty years has slowly bifurcated into the two groups described here. Traditional chaplaincy has retained its strong affiliation with religion, while professional chaplaincy has evolved to mirror the diversity found in society. For this group, chaplaincy has moved from an *occupation* to a *profession*.[27]

For a variety of reasons, attendance and participation in Christian churches began to decline in the 1960s. Some of the people who were part of that exodus discovered that what they had valued in Christianity began to be called "spirituality." Various spiritual exercises began to evolve, and spirituality lost its exclusive anchor in conventional religion. Chaplains learned not to dismiss these new experiences of spirituality.[28]

The contemporary chaplain is faced with traditional religion, new spiritualities, many faiths, and nonbelievers, as well as LGBTQIAP people and other aspects of diversity. Billings adds that, "Ministering to people who could come from any of these backgrounds might seem like mission impossible, but over the years, chaplaincy has evolved to do exactly that."[29] Chaplaincy has become a distinctive profession, open to practitioners with as varied a personal and spiritual background as the general public. Some may lament that chaplaincy appears to have become unmoored from its place as an affiliate of the Christian religion.

The emergence of professional chaplaincy has been in process for decades, and even those of us who were part of the transition did not always recognize it until some experience brought it into focus. My understanding of the distinction between traditional and professional chaplaincy came into focus in the mid-90s, when I served as a hospital chaplain. One occasion was a conversation with a visitor, who let me know that I did not meet her expectations.

Standing in the hallway outside the Intensive Care Unit, I noticed a woman who appeared to be lost. "Can I help you find something?" I asked. As she gave me the room number where her loved one had been transferred, her eyes went to my name badge. "Oh, you're a chaplain!" she exclaimed. "That's wonderful! I didn't think the hospital would allow ministers to visit patients." I told her that I was there to support all patients and visitors, regardless of whether they identified with a religious tradition or not. "What an opportunity," she said. "That's great! What a mission field."

"Well, no, this isn't a mission field," I said. "It's a hospital. I only visit people who want to see me. People are sick, and I wouldn't take advantage of their vulnerability by insisting on seeing people who don't want me there."

Her bright smile faded into a scowl. She turned and walked away, saying, "Oh, you're one of those. You sold out."

This is one place where the chaplaincy map shows diverging paths. Some chaplains and hiring organizations prefer the *traditional* model of chaplaincy.

The ranks of *professional* chaplains and the contexts in which they serve reveal a different perspective. Professional chaplaincy includes individuals from across the spectrum of world religious traditions and humanists. These chaplains may also come into the field from educational/professional backgrounds in nursing, social work, psychology, and other disciplines. They meet the educational and clinical training requirements for board certification and adhere to a code of ethics. A challenge for professional chaplaincy is "to show that chaplaincy not only contributes to the well-being of those who have faith, but also to others beyond the boundaries of faith."[30]

The Value of Modern Chaplaincy

The people making administrative and budget decisions about funding chaplaincy may weigh the business case, and find practical, functional arguments more persuasive. "In other words, people can see value in religion even if they are not people of faith themselves and could see value in funding chaplaincy where the resources it brings are seen to make a significant difference to the well-being of individuals and institutions."[31]

"The overarching justification for [funding] chaplaincy must be that it 'adds value'—it does something valuable that no other professional group does. It offers a form of care that is best captured by the terms 'spiritual' and 'pastoral,' and it is able to do this because gradually over the past half century or so chaplaincy has become a discrete professional group with its own skills and expertise."[32]

Drawing on Billings' work in "The Place for Chaplaincy in Public Life," I have identified the following ways in which chaplaincy adds value:[33]

Contemporary chaplains serve as "cultural brokers," helping an organization to be religiously and culturally literate and aware. The chaplain supports the organization through education and advocacy, both to honor and respect people and to avoid miscommunications and misunderstandings that can be hurtful.

Each year during EMS Week, picnics and barbecues are held at ambulance bases to celebrate "our" week. The food served at these events is determined by the host and usually consists of grilled meats—chicken, hamburgers, hot dogs, pork ribs.

Several years ago at an EMS Week picnic, the only meats on the table were hot dogs (containing pork), pulled pork sandwiches, and barbecued pork ribs. One of our guests was a Muslim colleague. I saw him pause as he looked over the food and then fill his plate with vegetables and salads and an empty bun.

This was not a case of deliberate exclusion and did not warrant a scold or admonishment. The issue was hospitality. We had invited the community to join us in celebration of EMS Week and had overlooked the dietary restrictions of one of our guests. I consulted with Jewish and Muslim chaplain colleagues about how to bring this to the attention of our leadership, and what suggestions to make. Substituting or including other foods, segregating the pork from other meats, and labeling the items on the serving table were simple and effective solutions.

Chaplains are expected to provide spiritual care to all, without constraints. They are granted access to people at every level of the organization. Critically, the chaplain is available for all. The nature of the care may be work-related or home-related. When a paramedic or dispatcher receives a promotion, celebration and congratulations are in order. But the competitive nature of promotions also includes those who are not chosen for a position to which they had aspired. On occasion, I have been aware of those who had interviewed for leadership positions, only to experience the disappointment that comes with not being selected. I made the effort to create a space for those individuals, recognizing the grief and reassessment that follows those losses. Personal events in the lives of employees such as births, deaths, graduations, weddings, and divorces all merit acknowledgment and support as well.

Specific examples of how chaplains add value will emerge in each context. The chaplain who is attentive to the stresses of the organization, and who takes the time to build relationships, will find that it is precisely at the critical moments that chaplaincy demonstrates its value. When an ambulance was involved in a head-on collision, seriously injuring the EMT and paramedic inside, I was integrally involved in the immediate and long-term response. The chief contacted me at 2:00 a.m. with a request to join him on a call to the employee's family, notifying them of the crash and critical injury of their loved one. The incident shook the field staff, many of whom spontaneously began gathering at the base the next day. I joined them and cofacilitated the crisis response, providing listening, support, and education.

On an individual level, when an employee mentioned the loss of a beloved pet, a simple act of compassion was received with gratitude.

Chaplains also recognize that while not everyone comes from a religious background, all human beings share a general need to find value, meaning, and purpose in their lives. The training and experience of chaplains gives them the relevant skills to be a resource in the task of meaning-making. This may emerge after a high-stress incident, or by asking about the most memorable calls an EMT or medic has been on, or what it was about a particular call that made it significant. Commonly, it is a meaningful interaction or personal connection that imprinted the call on the memory of the provider.

A growing body of research indicates that people's well-being is enhanced when physical, emotional, and spiritual needs are addressed together. Corporations are taking seriously the place of employee well-being. Attention to the whole person is credited with benefits to the organization such as improved employee retention, reduced absenteeism, and a more engaged workforce.

To speak only of employee retention, it has been estimated that the cost to an EMS agency to replace one paramedic is in the range of $72,000.[34] In addition to the financial costs when an employee leaves are the loss of cohesion and comradery among the ambulance crews. Efforts to create and nurture a culture of support impact the bottom line. Employee engagement, reduced turnover, and reduced absenteeism are seen to be indirect benefits of a chaplain for staff support.

For those who look for quantifiable measures, these "how chaplains add value" points may be sufficient reasons "why" an organization hires a chaplain in support of its employees. Yet my employers didn't hire me in order to obtain those things, and I'm not the only person who supports our employees. Chapter Two will illustrate that there are many others under that umbrella. This is a group effort. The "why" to this position remains "because we care about our employees."

EMS Chaplaincy: At the Intersection of Healthcare, Public Safety, and Workplace Chaplaincy

Healthcare, public safety, and workplace chaplaincy are the three legs of the EMS chaplaincy stool. Any framework for EMS chaplaincy will need to address these three realities. Each one goes to a fundamental feature of the world that frontline providers live in.[35]

- EMS is **healthcare** and needs to observe strict protocols from the medical director.
- EMS is **public safety**. Arriving on the scene of an emergency, EMTs and paramedics have regular interactions with law enforcement and fire department personnel, their public safety partners.

- EMS is a **workplace**. As with any other job, there are unique aspects of the workplace, and sometimes the stress of the job is the job itself.

When we discuss the issues faced by EMS professionals, they will line up under these three legs.

EMS chaplaincy, then, has some common features with:

- Healthcare chaplaincy—especially ED and ICU (trauma and critically ill patients). There is much in the literature that describes the identity, role, and function of the healthcare chaplain.

- Public safety chaplaincy—serving law enforcement and fire, these chaplains are in the public safety arena alongside EMS chaplains.
- Workplace chaplaincy—the primary constituency of the EMS chaplain is the employees, dealing with
  - Workplace issues (coworkers, managers, other job-related topics)
  - Home, family, and personal issues, similar to workplace chaplaincy in any setting
  - Work-related stresses specific to EMS

A few more words about workplace chaplaincy are in order. A person seeking to affiliate with a faith community has the option of choosing which congregation to join, and who to accept as their spiritual leader. The workplace is not a church, synagogue, or mosque. The chaplain is not the minister, priest, rabbi, or imam of a congregation. More will be said in Chapter Three about the relationship between the workplace chaplain and the employees of the workplace.

The point here is that employees do not generally have a voice in who is hired to be the organization's chaplain. Those decisions are made by administrators, following a Human Resources procedure. In the pluralistic context of the workplace, it is essential that the chaplain is able to articulate the theological foundations and scope of practice for their ministry, both for their own self-understanding as well as for the benefit of those among whom they work.

Effective chaplaincy ministry requires that the chaplain be clear about their purpose, goal, and foundations for being there. This is both a practical issue and an ethical mandate. In practical terms, disclosing one's role, purpose, and religious affiliation invites the other into relationship. It advances the work of assessing and addressing spiritual care needs. As an ethical mandate, the chaplain's transparency ensures that there is no hidden agenda. The recipient of the chaplain's care, including their religious and spiritual beliefs and practices, is given the honor and respect due any human being.

Chapter Two
"Why"

Core Motivations or Purposes for an EMS Organization to Employ a Chaplain

Critical incidents are often the catalyst for EMS agencies to consider hiring a chaplain, as a way to support their employees.

EMS chaplaincy exists because:

- EMS is a high-stress job. Our employees have a right to be supported.
- We care about our employees' emotional, mental, physical, and spiritual well-being.

Society holds in high regard those who do something extraordinary "because it's the right thing to do." Those who hold or manage financial resources are well-positioned to make things happen because of their belief that it's the right thing to do. Individuals and organizations on tight budgets may be forced to justify decisions that come with costs but with less measurable benefits to the bottom line. Without a clear commitment to the hiring and support for a chaplain, the position is at risk for being cut or downgraded if/when chaplain services are considered to be too expensive or nonessential.

Any organization grappling with the "why" statements above will be advised to take their time in deciding to hire a chaplain (or a person in any other discipline whose focus is on employee support). Issues to be considered include operational matters such as:

- Goals and expectations for the position
- Scope of practice and standard operating procedures
- Reporting relationships
- Performance evaluation plan
- Budget, including benefits, annual raises, and possible increase in the FTE
- Required credentials

Organizations need to be clear about their philosophy and priorities around emotional, psychological, and spiritual well-being. The leadership team needs to be on the same page about the issues, what services will be provided, how those services will be provided, and how success will be evaluated. Enthusiasm may lead to blind spots, and a chaplain may be recruited too soon. Without a full understanding of what the organization hopes to accomplish, there likely will be no agreement on the leadership team about why they are hiring a chaplain or what to expect from the person hired. The chaplain and the chaplain's performance can become the lightning rod for a program that is not fully formed.

The leadership team should be able to articulate the "why" to the workforce, as well as why the decision was made to hire a *chaplain* to perform those functions (as opposed to hiring a social worker or psychologist). Hiring should not take place until those decisions are made and questions about the position are answered. Occasionally a key person will decide for or against chaplaincy based on subjective or personal experience. Generally, I believe people in leadership roles are reasonable and will acknowledge that a particular budget item may benefit the organization even if they themselves are indifferent to it. On the other side of the interview table, applicants for chaplaincy positions are advised specifically to ask about organizational and senior leadership support for and commitment to the position. The burden of justifying the position should not fall on the chaplain.

These are issues I would advise any EMS agency considering hiring a chaplain to consider, and any chaplain interviewing for a job to ask. This is for the benefit of everyone—the board and leadership team of the employing organization, the chaplain being considered for the job, and perhaps most importantly, the rank-and-file employees we are here to support.

***

Much has been written about why organizational health is essential to the success of any business. Sinek's discussion of trust provides another perspective on why an EMS agency might consider hiring a chaplain. Think of this in terms of organizational culture. Trust is a performance category that is nearly impossible to measure.[36] Sinek writes that:

> *For those within a community, or an organization, they must trust that their leaders provide a net— practical or emotional. With that feeling of support, those in the organization are more likely to put in extra effort that ultimately benefits the group as a whole.*
>
> *Great organizations become great because the people inside the organization feel protected. People come to work knowing that their bosses, colleagues, and the organization as a whole will look out for them. This results in reciprocal behavior. Individual decisions, efforts, and behaviors support, benefit, and protect the long-term in-*

terest of the organization as a whole. [37]

One of the ways an organization can build and maintain an organizational culture based on trust, providing an emotional safety net, is by hardwiring employee well-being. A chaplain alone cannot do this; it takes a broad-based approach. Many of the items under the umbrella are already present. This focus here is on one of those, the EMS chaplain.

Employee Support

EMS chaplain	Supervisors and managers	Family, friends, community
Peer support team	Post-incident de-briefing	Professional therapy/counseling
Resiliency, suicide prevention	Employee Assistance Program (EAP)	Other related training and education

Setting Yourself Up for Success

Reactive crisis support sits alongside the proactive/self-directed nature of this position. The reactive part is fairly easy to see; the proactive responsibility cannot be overstated, nor can the amount of flexibility required for the job to be done well. The organization has to trust the chaplain to do their job, and the chaplain is obligated to honor that trust by maintaining the highest level of personal and professional integrity. The chaplain has to maintain a high degree of visibility among the workforce to build relationships and to be accessible. EMS is a 24/7 business, and the chaplain must work flexible hours, including visiting the base in the evenings and on weekends. A certain amount of credibility is granted to the chaplain, and a certain amount is earned. The chaplain demonstrates commitment to all of the crew members by supporting all of them, at all hours of the day or night, in all seasons and in all kinds of weather.

The caveat here is that no one is physically able or consciously expected to work 24/7. The chaplain needs a day off, and there will be periods when the chaplain is not available—especially if the position is less than full-time. Expectations must be clarified and transparent for the benefit of everyone. The good news is that the EMS chaplain does not usually need to drop everything and run. The immediate support needs of a crew that has been involved in a critical incident can be met by the duty officer or other operations leader. A more effective chaplaincy or mental health follow-up will take place 24–72 hours later, after the employee has had time to rest, eat, and begin to regain their sense of equilibrium.

The chaplain is responsible for negotiating all of this, both with the EMS leaders and with the chaplain's own family. Better to let the call go to voicemail than to answer the phone during a family gathering. And, once the chaplain has had a few minutes to listen to the message/read the email, the chaplain has to assess the urgency of the incident and decide when to reply. A supportive family may understand the need to make a short phone call, though everyone benefits from clear boundaries and backup on-call coverage provided by an EMS leader or a chaplain colleague when the chaplain is not available.

Two additional boundaries require clarification: death notifications, and whether the EMS chaplain will provide support to families, community members, and bystanders of critical incidents. In my clinical practice in healthcare, medical information is delivered by medical professionals and the chaplain is present to support people after they receive that information. I don't do death notifications. I recognize that my chaplain colleagues in military or other public safety contexts may have a different practice and rationale for doing so. Since there are medical professionals immediately available to provide information and answer questions, I believe delivering such news fits more in the scope of practice of the paramedic than of the EMS chaplain.

Regarding support to families and bystanders, when riding along with a crew, I am happy to provide whatever support I can while we are on scene. Beyond that, I defer to local resources and police/fire chaplains in the community.

***

EMS chaplains are unlikely to have anyone actively managing or directing their work, so must take the initiative in building and maintaining relationships. There may be few requests or referrals, and the people in the chaplain's care may be scattered across multiple sites, miles apart. Take every opportunity to connect—ride with ambulance crews, sit with dispatchers, attend leader meetings and length-of-service ceremonies. Schedule time with every member of the leadership team; ask them about the industry, current issues, and listen to their hopes and dreams for the organization.

Culture change can take years,[38] so shifting to an

intentional model of proactive employee support is a marathon, not a sprint. Any organization hiring their first chaplain will find itself in the same position. At the time I began as chaplain with Allina EMS, it didn't occur to me to ask for a five-year commitment to the position, how we would set goals, how I would be evaluated, or how we would know if the position was even viable. In retrospect, I realize that I knew I had my hospital job to fall back on and was oblivious to the culture change we were initiating. I hadn't really made a long-term commitment to EMS, either.

From the perspective of the employer, I would advise any organization that is considering hiring a chaplain to be aware that the chaplain alone will be a symbol of a culture change, and to move publicly toward that change. Likewise, I would encourage any chaplain interviewing for a position—especially with an organization that has never had a chaplain before—to discuss the long-term implications of having a chaplain in their midst. The workforce will recognize that things are changing and ask legitimate questions about the direction the organization is taking. Some may openly resist or oppose the change. Confusion about the need for a chaplain and whether it is a worthwhile budget item will surface. Employees may associate the chaplain with their previous experience with religion, and apply those assumptions and expectations to the EMS chaplain. As noted above, senior leaders' commitment to employee well-being and explicit support for the chaplain are essential.

Staffing

In order for the EMS chaplaincy program to succeed, the organization needs to make a long-term commitment to the position. A challenge to that commitment is the part-time nature of the job. Many EMS organizations will not have the budget or the need for a full-time position. Hiring a chaplain at half time or less means the person in the job will likely need another source of income. Like the paramedic who works for more than one ambulance service, many chaplains have more than one job. Potential EMS chaplains may also work in hospitals, mental health clinics, or congregations. It may also be an attractive option for chaplains who prefer a part-time job while they have children at home, pursue other interests, or meet other obligations.

Like any relationship between organization and employee, an EMS chaplaincy program has some essential tasks for each party. I have identified three core needs for each. The organization needs to:

- Define clear goals and expectations
- Trust in the chaplain as a professional

- Provide support for the chaplain

For the chaplain, the roadmap to a successful launch includes:
- Self-initiative
- Flexibility
- High visibility

Evidence-Based Professional Practice

My observations about how EMS providers cope with the stress of the job led to some questions and hunches. I wondered, *how do people shift from merely coping to actually growing into their profession? Is there more to it than experience and supportive friends?* This led to two research studies.

Professional chaplains are turning to original research to provide the foundations for clinical practice. Though measurement tools are not commonly associated with the work of the EMS chaplain, our work can be informed by the intentional use of research methods. The well-being initiative at Allina Health EMS is an example of how this can be done.

The position of EMS chaplain was new when I started in 2007. I wondered how I would determine who had experienced a difficult call and how to prioritize them. I asked the operations leaders what types of calls were most likely to cause distress and used their top-ten list to develop standard operating procedures for when we asked leaders to notify the EMS chaplain.

1. Any event that results in a Critical Incident Stress Debriefing (CISD), even if no one from our organization participates
2. Death of a child
3. Multiple casualty incidents
4. Fatalities resulting from fires
5. Two or more high-stress calls in the same shift
6. Employee assaulted by a patient
7. Traumatic work-related injury
8. Line-of-duty death
9. High-stress phone calls impacting dispatch staff
10. Grotesque injuries or deaths such as decapitation, dismemberment, or burned beyond recognition

This list was the beginning of the journey to create an evidence-based EMS chaplaincy practice and led to two Institutional Review Board (IRB)[39]-approved studies. I was primary investigator for the first, a cross-sectional, validated survey of Allina dispatchers, EMTs, and paramedics to evaluate professional burnout and an extensive list of potential risk factors. Survey respondents indicated that they perceived critical incidents involving children to be among the most difficult to experience and cope with. All seven of the pediatric incident types presented in the survey had very high average severity ratings and accounted for seven of the top eight event types rated most difficult to cope with.

This is evidence, provided by our own clinicians: pediatric calls are among the most difficult calls they get. This is not new. We know that calls involving children are challenging. When a call came in of a fourteen-year-old who had fallen through the ice on a local lake, there was a heightened sense of awareness and concern on the part of our staff, and expressions of support for the crew who responded, one of whom had a fourteen-year-old.

During my residency at the trauma hospital, I responded to a call in which a six-year-old boy had been brought in. He and his friends were playing Peter Pan, jumping on the bed in a second-floor bedroom, pretending to fly. He flew across the room and hit the screen on the window; the screen popped out. A neighbor saw him fly out the window and land on the concrete patio. A large family group followed the ambulance to the hospital. After getting the family situated in the waiting room, I found a quiet spot where I could call home. My daughters were both preschoolers at the time. "Hello," my wife answered the phone. "Hi," I replied, "how is everyone doing this afternoon?" She got it. She understood. "We're fine. What just happened at the hospital?" I told her we had admitted a young boy, I couldn't give her any details, but I just needed to make sure everyone at home was all right.

As it turned out, the patient had no concussion, no bleeds, no breaks, and no sprains. Apparently he did everything right, by instinct. He relaxed as he flew through the air, tucked his head, and rolled. In some ways, though, it doesn't matter what the outcome was. I would have cried anyway, just thinking about what could have happened. When I got home that afternoon, my children got an extra-long hug. A few years later, I cut the cartoon on the next page out of the paper and have had it on my bulletin board for the past twenty-five years. My EMS colleagues understand.

Consistent with our findings and irrespective of methods or geography, studies universally report that calls involving children or persons personally or professionally known to the crew are among the most disturbing. Unique to the current study, however, was an examination of incident severity rating by parental status. We hypothesized that emergency responders with children might find pediatric critical incidents more distressing because of mental and emotional transference of the situation to children in their own lives; that had been my personal experience. But our findings did not support any difference in perceived severity by parental status.[40]

In other words, it doesn't matter if the provider is a parent or not. Pediatric calls can be distressing to anyone. Informed by this evidence, I adapted my chaplaincy practice to place a high priority on follow-up contacts to all paramedics, EMTs, and dispatchers who were involved in code three, lights-and-sirens, emergency transports of pediatric patients.

Our research team also conducted a follow-up focus group study to further delve into what specific elements of pediatric calls contribute to distress. The findings have been published in two peer-reviewed papers to date.

The first, "Burnout and Exposure to Critical Incidents in a Cohort of Emergency Medical Services Workers from Minnesota,"[41] provides quantitative data on EMS providers' exposure to critical incidents.

The second, "Emergency Medical Services Provider Perspectives on Pediatric Calls: A Qualitative Study,"[42] summarizes the qualitative information gleaned from the follow-up focus groups.

Future Research

The next step in this process has been to identify and refine the referrals from supervisors and managers informing me of high-stress calls involving children, as well as referrals for follow-ups based on other criteria. Sometimes employees will contact me directly, on behalf of a coworker or to request support for themselves.

Another source of information about calls involving pediatric patients is the use of an automated notification program, set up through the communications center. Using keywords, the FirstWatch program generates email reports informing me of calls that meet the established criteria.

The initial notification gives basic information, such as the nature of the call, location, and crew members. After the patient care report is submitted, I receive that narrative as well. Within hours, usually before the end of the shift, I have sufficient information to begin reaching out to the dispatcher and crew members. With both human and electronic referrals, the chaplain's work is reactive, responding to requests and referrals.

We have yet to do the work of measuring the impact of the chaplains' care. In many ways, discovering the evidence on which to focus the EMS chaplain's work has been the easy part. Measuring its effectiveness will be a greater challenge.

Chapter Three
"How"*

Guiding Values and Principles

This chapter will discuss the values of
1. Show up (a ministry of presence)
2. Speak up (professional values and principles)
3. Lift up (listening, encouraging, affirming)

Show Up:
A Ministry of Presence

My Clinical Pastoral Education residency year was at a Level 1 trauma hospital. The department secretary did not have a spiritual care background. She was hired to provide administrative support to the team of

---

*Simon Sinek defines the "how" as values or principles that guide how you bring your cause to life. Values have to be verbs.

staff chaplains, volunteer chaplains, CPE supervisor, and students. One day she commented that in her observation, "You guys don't do any work! You just walk around the hospital all day and talk to people!" We tried, with limited success, to explain to her that walking around the hospital talking to people *is* the chaplain's work.

Paget and McCormack, chaplains and seminary professors, write in *The Work of the Chaplain* that:

> *Chaplain ministry has often been called the "ministry of presence." Presence is both physical and emotional. First, the chaplain makes a conscious choice to be physically present with the client. Second, the chaplain is emotionally present with the client through empathetic listening. Through presence, the chaplain begins to build the relationship that eventually brings comfort to those who feel alone in their suffering or despair.*
>
> *Some become frustrated with the ministry of presence. Goals don't seem to get accomplished. Tasks don't seem important. Doing seems secondary to being. Both the chaplain and the public may perceive that nothing is happening. But for the experienced spiritual care provider, the art of "hanging out" with patients, victims, cli-*

ents, or team members becomes an intentional event that leads to providing a calm presence during times of stress or chaos.

The law enforcement chaplain practices intentional presence—"loitering with intent" to calm, to build relationships, to provide compassion. The healthcare chaplain practices patient presence (in both senses of the word!)—serenely listening to the same narrative of diagnosis, treatment, and recuperative concerns. The crisis intervention or disaster relief chaplain practices "non-anxious presence"—demonstrating no anxiety or panic about the bombing, about the flooding, about destruction left by fires, tornadoes, hurricanes, or tsunamis.

The ministry of presence often looks like standing around the water cooler, circulating among the people, sitting quietly with someone, or having a cup of coffee in the lunchroom. Presence may seem insignificant, but presence is the grace gift that chaplains bring to the human encounter. It is being available in spite of other commitments.[43]

While "presence" is certainly central to chaplaincy practice, it is a process or an intervention, not an outcome. The chaplain is present in order for something else to happen. Presence is great as a matter of clinical practice, but it has to produce something.

> *I've learned that people will forget what you said, people will forget what you did, but people will never forget how you made them feel.*
>
> — *Maya Angelou* —

A crew called me around midnight. They were at the scene of a residence where a man had come home from work and discovered that his wife had died. The crew confirmed the death and was preparing to leave but were concerned about him being there alone as he waited for the mortuary staff. Was I available to come? On one hand, it wasn't part of my scope of practice to support families and community members. But their concern for the family was clear. I knew that there would be a police officer present until the hearse came, so it wasn't a safety concern. I said yes. The crew thanked me for coming, notified the dispatcher that they were clearing the scene, and departed. I sat and talked with the grieving widower for a while, listening as he struggled to make meaning out of his experience that evening. It was a ministry of presence, both to him and to the ambulance crew, who expressed their gratitude for my response.

Paramedics, EMTs, dispatchers, wheelchair van drivers—all who touch the lives of patients—confront human suffering on a routine basis. Our immediate focus may be on the physical, clinical needs of the patients, yet we are profoundly aware that the most powerful tool we have for the care of others is our human presence. EMS personnel are drawn to this work by something almost beyond words. I believe it is hope. There is no reason to put ourselves in situations of tragedy and pain without some sense of hope for the future, which we strive to improve.

***

Cumulative stress, critical incidents, and the emotional weight of our work are familiar to all of us whose jobs involve caring for people in crisis. We know how important it is to be deliberate about having a life outside of work, tending to our personal relationships, eating healthy food, exercising, and getting enough sleep. So it may come as a surprise when we begin to notice that we're not bothered as much by difficult cases as we used to be. A nineteen-year fire EMT came up to me during a break at a conference. He described having clear memories of a terrible call he was on more than a dozen years ago, while the details of a more recent, equally challenging call were not so clear. He asked, "Am I getting cold and calloused? Should I be concerned?" These are common questions.

In reply, I asked if he had normal emotional responses to events when he wasn't at work. "Oh yes," he said. "I cry at funerals, I teared up with joy at my son's wedding." I assured him that I didn't have any concerns about him, but if he was still worried about it, it would be a good topic to explore with a trained therapist.

An adult patient was coding in the hospital ICU. His frightened brother noticed that I was able to be at the bedside without appearing to be in much distress myself. He commented, "I suppose this kind of work gets easier over time." Easier? No, I told him, it doesn't get easier, but it does get more familiar. This is also true for those who work in EMS, be it trauma, interfacility, community paramedic, dispatcher, or chaplain.

One of the things I've come to recognize is that our responses to stress involve more than one emotion. A normal response to loss is to feel grief or sadness, a typical response to trauma is to be afraid, and all of that intense emotion can be overwhelming. With experience, the "fear factor" is less than it used to be. Situations that used to scare me aren't so scary anymore. I still experience some initial anxiety as I make the mental shift necessary to respond to a crisis. I notice a heightened sense of awareness, faster heartbeat, and other physical responses, but I'm not as frightened. I observe my EMS coworkers responding in much the same way.

We grow into our professions. With experience and support from coworkers, family, and friends, we can increase our skill at coping with stress and trauma. The fear element is reduced. We have a broader base of experience to draw on, and even though the current situation isn't exactly the same as something we've seen before, we gain confidence in our abilities. It's not easier, but it is more familiar.

And yet, there are times when even the most seasoned professional faces a situation that catches them off guard. Without asking for details, bring up the topic of the most memorable call and watch the heads nod.

One late December night, I was on call for the hospital and received a page at 2:00 a.m. A man had been brought in via ambulance; I met his wife in the waiting room. She said she had been finishing up some laundry after her husband had gone to bed. They had family coming from out of state to celebrate the holidays. Suddenly her husband began throwing up and screaming in pain. It was a chaotic scene. She called 911 and quickly made arrangements for a friend to watch her children. Now she was at the hospital, anxious to hear news of what had happened. I walked with her to meet the doctor, where she learned that her husband had had a brain aneurysm and would not survive. The family coming for Christmas would be coming to his funeral.

About this time, I became aware that I was shutting down emotionally. In the face of an incredibly sad and painful situation, I felt nothing. In my confusion, I decided that it was probably OK that I didn't feel anything, because I had work to do. I helped her make some phone calls, accompanied her to the ICU to see her husband, and got her something warm to drink and a blanket so she could try to rest.

By the time I was ready to leave, I had been there an hour and a half; it was after 3:30. I was exhausted. Fortunately, I live only three miles from the hospital and it was the middle of the night, because I was four blocks away from the hospital when the tears started. I felt a wave roll over me, as all of the emotions flooded in. My body had given me ninety minutes when the physical and emotional pain was blocked, and I didn't feel anything. I realized that the patient was close to my own age, his children a few years older than mine. He had family coming from out of state; my family was already here, sleeping at my house. I drove very slowly, blinking back the tears, arrived safely at home, shut off the car, and sobbed.

A colleague observed that in trauma work, first you bury your parents, then your spouse, then your children, then your friends, and then you bury yourself. Not literally, of course, but in the sense that we care for patients who remind us of someone we know and care about, and I am confronted with the hard reality that I could lose one of my loved ones. Sometimes it's like looking in the mirror, when I realize that this could be me. It happens to all of us, and it's normal.

On another occasion, I drove home in the rain after riding along with a crew on an evening shift. When I pulled up in front of my garage, the garage door opener didn't work. I parked the car, got out in the pouring rain, walked around the garage, and in the side door. After parking inside, I got out, now soaking wet. It occurred to me that this was only an inconvenience. We had had a couple of difficult calls that evening. The worst thing that happened to me that day was that I got wet. Strange as it might seem, doing this work has filled me with a deep sense of gratitude. I hear stories like this from some of the people I work with. Facing the fragility of life every day can contribute to a more profound sense of gratitude, leading to a deeper appreciation for the ordinary.

***

Professionals working in healthcare settings are more visible than they sometimes realize. For eight years I worked half-time in EMS and half-time in the hospital. The contrast between the two settings was striking. For one, the hospital is a fairly controlled environment, with rules about who can enter the patient's room. Street medics, on the other hand, grow accustomed to the bystanders. Whether in a private residence, a place of business, or on the side of the road, there are likely to be people standing and watching. A hospital nurse colleague championed the idea of allowing family members to be present during a code, when a patient was being resuscitated. Together with an interdisciplinary team, we worked for ten years to bring about a culture change in the hospital. The process involved research, presentations, and proposed procedures to address the concerns of physicians and others who resisted the idea. Finally the practice was accepted, and families were allowed to be present. My EMS colleagues listened to those stories and shook their heads.

A senior medic described the time he was at a hardware store on his day off, in street clothes, when another shopper recognized him. She said he had saved her son's life several years before and proceeded to introduce the boy to the paramedic. The paramedic had to admit that he did not remember the incident, though he was gracious about it and thanked her for stopping to tell him.

Metaphors and Chaplaincy

The metaphors we use not only reflect, but also influence, the way we think about a topic.[44] In terms of the chaplain's place in the EMS organization, the metaphor of "family" provides a glimpse of how the chaplain resembles an in-law. Some fire and law enforcement departments and EMS agencies use the "family" metaphor in reference to the entire organization. The picture of a family implies feelings of connectedness, support, and nurturing.

The image of a family can be used in different ways. Usually this term suggests an immediate family of two to three generations in which most members know each other. As organizations grow, the image of family might be stretched to include cousins and distant relatives who may only see each other occasionally, don't know each other, and have to rely on name tags.

In terms of the day-to-day work group, fire department personnel work in larger groups and may carry the "family" idea forward into their work relationships, referring to the team of coworkers who interact closely during the workday. This image may also apply to emergency dispatchers, who may share a common space and interact closely as they carry out their responsibilities.

Police often work alone, sometimes in pairs. Ambulance-based EMTs and paramedics also work in pairs, suggesting a metaphor of siblings or a "work spouse" relationship.

The public safety chaplain, including the EMS chaplain, may be likened to an in-law, welcomed from outside, allowed into the group at the invitation of a key member, but always occupying a place on the margins. However, as former chaplain and professor of theology Stephen Pattison observes, "It may be that marginality is one of the strengths of chaplaincy. Not only does it not promote [religion], chaplains only exist at the pleasure and with the patronage of host organizations. Thus they pose no real threat to their hosts and their practices, and they cannot be dominant or coercive. Chaplaincy in its marginal form is exactly the form of religious presence that is acceptable in secular institutions."[45]

Speaking of the chaplain as "marginalized" is descriptive of the chaplain's place in the organization. Chaplains are well aware of their place in a hierarchical structure. Thus it came as little surprise when I encountered this perception in a community setting.

The service area for Allina EMS includes the Minneapolis–St. Paul Airport. People who work at the airport are required to take a class and pass a background check to get a badge allowing them into secure areas of the airport, places that are off limits to the public. In order to accompany paramedics in response to medical emergencies at the airport, I wear a security badge, which must be renewed annually.

To my embarrassment, I procrastinated on getting my security badge renewed, and there wasn't time to schedule an appointment with the airport police. I had to go as a walk-in, which meant getting in a queue and waiting, possibly for four or five hours. One of the EMS managers suggested wearing my uniform to the badging office and going directly to Station 7, where I might be able to get an expedited process. It had worked for paramedics.

So I was hopeful when the attendant smiled and asked if she could help me. I explained that I needed to renew my badge and inquired as to the process for doing so. She said "Yes, of course. Are you a paramedic?" "No," I replied, "I'm the EMS chaplain and provide support to the paramedics."

In a matter-of-fact tone, she told me to get in the queue, that someone would be glad to assist me when my number was called.

The Metaphor of the Good Samaritan

The history of EMS includes references to the biblical story of the Good Samaritan.

> *There was once a man traveling from Jerusalem to Jericho. On the way he was attacked by robbers. They took his clothes, beat him up, and went off, leaving him half dead. Luckily, a priest was on his way down the same road, but when he saw him he angled across to the other side. Then a Levite religious man showed up; he also avoided the injured man.*
>
> *A Samaritan traveling the road came on him. When he saw the man's condition, his heart went out to him. He gave him first aid, disinfecting and bandaging his wounds. Then he lifted him onto his donkey, led him to an inn, and made him comfortable. In the morning he took out two silver coins and gave them to the innkeeper, saying, "Take good care of him. If it costs any more, put it on my bill—I'll pay you on my way back."* [46]

EMS bears the image of the Samaritan in several ways.

First, the Samaritan acknowledges the inherent

worth and great value of the one stripped, beaten, and then left for half dead, not mindful of his identity or race. Despite the animosity between peoples, the Samaritan rendered a healing service using all his capacity under the circumstances, showing mercy and compassion.

EMS is caregiving outside of society's usual parameters, given wherever the need exists, not limited to any particular community. It is a service associated with compassion, love, humility, self-sacrifice, generosity, and courage.

Second, the Samaritan exemplifies the courageous commitment to be vulnerable to risk, which is often a context of EMS. What if the robbers were still in the area? It would be possible that the Samaritan could become another victim. However, he accepted this risk by offering to help the fallen man. While safety is a priority in EMS, EMTs, paramedics, and dispatchers are prepared to take measured risks in stepping into situations that have an element of uncertainty. They allow themselves to be vulnerable to the emotional risk of caring for patients whose identities or circumstances may be uncomfortable, patients who may not survive, patients and families who remind them of their own loved ones, but whose humanity compels EMS professionals to put their patients' needs above their own.

Third, an important image in the story of the Samaritan is the inn. The inn is a temporary lodging place, a place where a journeying person finds room for the night. The Samaritan continued his journey but brought with him the wounded person. The next morning, he entrusted the man to the innkeeper, together with money from his own pocket. The inn and the innkeeper imply the interconnection of EMS with other healthcare disciplines, as part of the whole healthcare system.

Fourth, EMS goes beyond boundaries, as does the Samaritan. In the story, Samaritans were considered the outcasts. In this context, the Samaritan had a good reason to simply walk away. Yet, when the Samaritan saw the wounded man, he felt pity on him. The Samaritan—and the EMS professional—demonstrate that valuing a person is not determined by race, gender, religion, or social status, but that every person is worthy to receive care.

Lastly, the Samaritan in the story completed his journey while meeting the need of a wounded and marginalized person. The Samaritan did not give everything away. He did not abandon or neglect his own self. He loved himself, and he loved his neighbor. This was expressed in his words, "Take care of him; and whatever more you spend, I will repay you when I come back."

EMS is not self-negligence. The Samaritan did what was in his power to do, and then transferred care to the innkeeper. He went on his way, practicing good self-care.[47]

This story inspired laws known as Good Samaritan laws across the United States, protecting from liability those bystanders who stop and help someone in need of urgent care.

Know Who You Are: Metaphors for Professional Chaplaincy

The Witness

The image of the chaplain as witness comes from a legal context and describes one who has knowledge of something by recollection or experience, and who can tell about it accurately. Psychotherapist Kristi Pikiewicz writes that, "Bearing witness is a term that, used in psychology, refers to sharing our experiences with others, most notably in the communication to others of traumatic experiences."[48] The chaplain bears witness to the experiences of the EMS provider, affirming that the event really happened, corroborating the story. Bearing witness does not assume any pathology; there is nothing "wrong" with someone who experiences trauma, and there is nothing to "fix." Rather, the role of the witness is to provide a safe place to process the activities that occur in the normal course of the job, which sometimes carry a significant amount of emotional weight. It consists of giving and receiving empathy and support, lightening the emotional load, and may be verbal or unspoken, a ministry of presence.

The Sherpa

Sherpas are an ethnic people from the mountainous region in the Himalayas. The Western concept of a Sherpa is that of a guide and supporter for mountain climbers seeking to ascend Chomolungma (Mt. Everest). Sherpas are primarily known for their gracious hospitality. They may provide guidance and insight about the terrain, listening carefully and making suggestions for the well-being of the traveler.

Despite the expertise and experience of the Sherpa, they cannot climb for the ones making their own journey. However, the Sherpa can be a witness to this experience. Many people spend years preparing for a climb to the summit of Mt. Everest, only to reach the top without family or friends present. It is in this sacred moment that the Sherpa can be present.

Kiersten Jarvis observes that the relationship between the Sherpa and the traveler can be a metaphor for the relationship between the chaplain and the care receiver. Chaplains can offer support and accompany those on a literal or symbolic journey. They may be present for those whose family and friends are not immediately available, or who are emotionally unable to bear the weight of the story of a traumatic experience. In this space, the chaplain can become a bearer and giver of blessings through compassionate listening, quiet presence, and offering themselves as a witness.[49] Some of my colleagues in hospital and long-term care chaplaincy lived this out during the pandemic, when they were present with patients dying of COVID, whose loved ones were unable to be with them due to visiting restrictions.

The Accompanist

To accompany is to keep company with someone. It is also to play a supporting role on a musical instrument for someone taking the solo part, such as singing a song. Chaplain and musician Karen Hanson writes that the musical accompanist serves the singer and the song, listening carefully and following where it leads. Sometimes the accompanist picks up a theme and plays what they have heard or gives it a slightly different interpretation. Sometimes the singer takes the song in a new direction, and the accompanist follows as best they can.

The same skills figure in chaplaincy. Caring means playing a supportive role. It involves being actively engaged, being present in the here and now, listening carefully, paying attention, and helping the song emerge in its fullness. The musical accompanist may have strong feelings about how a song should be performed. The task, however, is to listen and respond appropriately, not to push for a particular outcome. The same holds true for the chaplain. The EMS chaplain accompanies ambulance crews and dispatchers, listening carefully, picking up themes as the EMS professional engages in the work of making meaning out of their experiences. That work may involve affirming, asking clarifying questions, or suggesting a slightly different interpretation. Like the musical accompanist, the chaplain's task is to listen and respond appropriately, following where the soloist leads.[50]

The Comet

One way to picture the relationship between the chaplain and the care receiver—or the patient and the EMS provider—is to use the image of the solar system. The care receiver is in the position of the sun, surrounded by circles of support. The inner rings may be compared to Mercury and Venus, representing immediate family and friends. The third ring, Earth, represents the support of coworkers, supervisors, and managers. Mars, Jupiter, and Saturn represent community-based support resources, including faith groups, congregations, social service agencies, and mental health providers. The role of the chaplain may sometimes resemble the support of the employing organization. The chaplain's position relative to the EMT, paramedic, or dispatcher may also be more akin to that of the relationship between the EMS professional and the patient—more like a comet, with its elliptical orbit—sometimes very close to the person in need, and then, when the crisis has passed, moving so far away as not to be noticed.

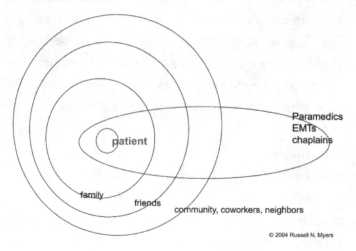

© 2004 Russell N. Myers

The Bearer of Bad News

Chaplains are sometimes mistaken for the Angel of Death or the Grim Reaper. This may come out of individual experience or from portrayals of chaplains in movies or television. It happens quickly and seems to be a subconscious reaction, with a variation on the question, "What do you know that I don't know, and who sent you?" When time and circumstances permit, the chaplain can speak to the uncertainty and assure the person that their role is not to bring news, but to bring support. Unfortunately, the perception of the chaplain as the bearer of bad news is sometimes so automatic and so powerful that there is little or nothing that can change it.

I was riding with one of the supervisors when we responded to a suicide call. As might be expected, it was tragic. The young man's mother thought he was at school. She came home and found him on his bedroom floor. I saw enough to know that there was no way he would survive the resuscitation efforts. Outside, she was pacing back and forth in the driveway, on the phone with her husband. We could hear her telling him that she needed him to come home, that it was urgent. She appeared to be too rational for the situation, though she was walking stiffly, and I wondered if she might need medical care herself.

The police saw that I was present, and gently suggested to her that the chaplain was here if she would like to talk. When she turned to look at me, her eyes grew wide and a look of horror came over her face. "Nooooo!" she screamed and began crying. I knew that I represented something to her, something she did not want to face. A woman appeared beside her (we learned that she was a neighbor) and put her arms around the grieving mother and let her cry. While I was helpless to console her, I took some comfort in knowing that she had a friend to be with her in that time of profound grief and loss.

Another form of "bad news" is when the chaplain is seen as the morality police. A group of people are talking and laughing, when one of them sees the chaplain approaching. Nonverbal cues are exchanged, and the conversation goes quiet, until someone awkwardly says, "Hi, Chaplain!" Or someone lets an expletive slip, then apologizes. Or they might deliberately use a four-letter word, pausing to see if they get a reaction from the chaplain. It all goes with the territory and most chaplains don't take it personally. One way I have found to address the issue proactively is by addressing the topic of alcohol use during the new employee academy. The message is simple and direct: I'm not the morality police. If you choose to use alcohol, that's your choice. What I will say is to be smart about it. Don't drink in a public place in uniform, and don't drink and drive. You will lose your job.

Metaphors for Congregation-Based Clergy that Do Not Fit for Chaplains

Public safety, by necessity, is a hierarchical structure. Chain of command is vital in responding to a crisis. In this context, the chaplain is one with no formal authority, suggesting a companionship. Using the metaphor of a corporate boardroom, the chaplain would be the one with "voice but no vote."

Following are two brief discussions of metaphors common in congregational ministry that do not fit for chaplains. These are offered as illustrations of metaphors that can lead to friction and frustration on the part of the chaplain, other professional staff, and the institution itself. The underlying issue here is the chaplain's self-identity. A risk for congregation-based clergy moving into chaplaincy without clinical training is the potential for conflict arising out of the chaplain's subconscious expectations.

Early in my chaplaincy career, I had colleagues who stepped on a few of these symbolic land mines. When things blew up, they were surprised and bewildered by the reaction of the hospital staff and administration. It was painful to watch and messy to clean up. Importantly, it was also avoidable and unnecessary, largely the result of misplaced metaphors.

The Parental Authority

In the congregational setting, the spiritual leader generally does have authority, which may include authority over programs, personnel, and budget. In some traditions, the image of family is used to describe the community of faith, and the minister has a parental role. In some instances this role gives the minister a degree of power. However, as anyone who has parented teens might recognize, parental authority changes when the teen no longer grants the parent the same degree of authority they once did. The parental authority may then be limited to persuasion.

Chaplain Jane Ellen Mauldin writes that, "The terms of the pastoral encounter are grounded in the other person's willingness to grant me authority to be their chaplain... I... enter with a sense of internal authority, the knowledge that I have skills and experience that some people find useful as they struggle with grief, loss, life changes, and ethical decision-making. However, the authority that really matters... is whatever authority [the other person] grants me as their chaplain... The authority is relational... That pastoral authority is activated daily by those who authorize me to be their chaplain."[51]

The relational nature of the chaplain's authority also means that some people do not authorize me to be their chaplain. They may relate to me as a friend, coworker, or in some other way, but if they withhold authorization, I cannot relate to them as their chaplain.

The Shepherd

From Chaplain Nathan Meskinoff's perspective, "Shepherding and other similar metaphors for chaplaincy often assign a privileged position to chaplains and their supposed wisdom... Such a position may be more appropriate to parish ministers and other settled clergy, who are, in most traditions, seen explicitly as a guide for the perplexed, offering instruction in how to walk the path of a particular tradition...

"The metaphor of the chaplain or minister as parent certainly has a long history... But while this is perhaps better than the image of the chaplain as shepherd... it still implies strongly that authority and wisdom lie within the chaplain."[52]

Know Where You Stand: Grounded in Tradition, Open to the World

While drawn from the Christian tradition, J. Philip Newell's perspective is easily adaptable to the chaplain of any religion or philosophy.[53] Newell uses the words *universal* and *particular* to describe his "two ways of listening."

The *universal* is expressed in the New Testament (Christian scriptures) Gospel of John, which he calls the John tradition. John's gospel opens with, "In the beginning was the Word, and the Word was with God, and the Word was God."

The *particular* is called the Peter tradition. The Peter tradition finds its greatest expression in the Gospel of Matthew, which opens with a lineage tracing Jesus' ancestry. Newell writes that:

> *The strength of the John tradition is that it produces a spirituality that sees God in the whole of life and regards all things as interrelated... John's way of seeing makes room for an open encounter with the Light of life wherever it is to be found... it is a tradition that can stand free of the four walls of the [congregation], for the sanctuary of God is not separate from but contained within the whole of creation.*
>
> *The strength of the Peter tradition is precisely that it does have four walls, as it were. It enshrines the Light of truth within the [faith community] and its traditions and sacraments... It allows us... to turn with faith to the familiar house of prayer where our mothers and fathers and those before them have for centuries found truth and guidance.*
>
> *These ways of seeing can combine to create a*

spirituality that is simultaneously well-rooted in a specific tradition and open to God in the whole of life. Together they can provide access to the ancient treasury of the house of faith, while at the same time equipping us to discern God's presence in all life. If they are not held together, however, the result will be a spirituality in part cut off from the world and, in its religious constraints, separated from life, from the earth and its people... Alternatively, the division might produce a spirituality that, in an attempt to broaden its vision, is no longer connected to any [religion] and becomes cut off from the truths and mysteries traditionally protected by the walls of the [faith community].[54]

Newell points to the need to hold differing perspectives in tension and is writing about spirituality. I see this as a model for a component of a theology or philosophy of chaplaincy as well. We are challenged to articulate our philosophy or theology of chaplaincy if we expect to be taken seriously as professional chaplains. We must both be grounded in our world view/faith tradition *and* open to seeing the divine in all people.

I don't really care what you believe, but *you* need to know. The chaplain's beliefs, world view, and biases will become apparent to the recipients of the chaplain's care. Chaplains who lack that self-awareness do a disservice to themselves, the care receiver, and the discipline of professional chaplaincy. It is no surprise that the first competency that candidates for board certification by the Association of Professional Chaplains (APC) are asked to address is to "Articulate an approach to spiritual care, rooted in one's faith/spiritual tradition that is integrated with a theory of professional practice."[55]

Those who minimize the value of identifying with a specific religion might lean toward the "John" tradition with its broad and universal perspective. Those who find themselves on the "Peter" end of the scale might be more at home within their own communities. I advocate for holding the two in tension. Either perspective, by itself, is incomplete. The notion of either/or does not and cannot work: both are highly valued and serve each other. Having a clear identity provides the chaplain with the foundation out of which to be open to the world. Being open to the world motivates the chaplain to clarify their own particular world view.

One way to think about this tension between the universal and the particular is to reframe it as world view. I may be open to the world, but except for short trips abroad have lived my entire life in the United States, and most of my adult life in the upper Midwest state of Minnesota. Thus, my "particular" viewpoint is from this context, whether I choose to acknowledge it or not. At the same time, in the context in which I live and work, I have interactions with people of a variety of religious and cultural traditions. Thus I am invited into a "universal" chaplaincy that sees God in the whole of life and regards all things as interrelated. This self-understanding enhances the chaplain's capacity to be fully present with those who come into the chaplain's care.

Speak up:
Professional Values and Principles

Respect

Many chaplaincy encounters occur at times of grief, loss, and vulnerability. A core value of EMS clinicians toward patients and others (families, bystanders, public safety partners) is respect. That same core value is also present in the relationship between the chaplain and the providers. This is particularly the case in circumstances of critical incident or cumulative stress, when field staff and dispatchers' vulnerability is heightened due to exposure to emotionally challenging situations. The chaplain who recognizes the need and opportunity to provide support is bound by a code of ethics that demands showing respect.

The chaplain may provide support in the form of prevention (establishing a supportive relationship), intervention (a ministry of presence or other active participation), or *postvention* (listening, debriefing, education). In any of those scenarios, respect is the only acceptable posture. Respect is shown in every aspect of the relationship and is expected from personnel of all disciplines. The benefit to having a formal, transparent ethical standard is that it protects everyone. The chaplain is conscious of this expectation, and the care receivers can be confident that it will be upheld. In the rare event that it is not, there is no ambiguity about whether a line has been crossed, and appropriate disciplinary action toward the chaplain is warranted.

Implications for EMS lie in the courtesy and respect shown by the clinicians to all who are in their care. I admire the professionalism of the paramedics, EMTs, and dispatchers who show no partiality in their care for the poor, the homeless and marginalized, the patients who request care on a frequent basis, and those whose definition of an emergency is much lower than that of the provider.

Hospitality

Hospitality is a foundational value in all relationships. Hospitality itself has its foundations in a theology of creation, which holds that all people are created equal, and sees the essential goodness in every person.

In his New Year message for 2001/5762, given a few days after the terrorist attacks on 9/11/2001, Sir Jonathan Sacks, chief rabbi of the United Hebrew Congregations of the Commonwealth, said that:

> *I used to think that the greatest command in the Bible was, "You shall love your neighbor as yourself." I was wrong. Only in one place does the Bible ask us to love our neighbor. In more than thirty places it commands us to love the stranger... It isn't hard to love our neighbors because by and large our neighbors are people like us. What's tough is to love the stranger, the person who isn't like us, who has a different skin color, or a different faith, or a different back-ground. That's the real challenge.*[56]

The roles of guest and host are exchanged, sometimes confused. When an ambulance crew enters the home of a patient, we are the guests in their space. When the patient is brought into the ambulance, the crew becomes the host and the patient is the guest in "our" space. Then if I, as EMS chaplain, move to the bedside to offer comfort and support, I enter the personal space of the patient, and become their guest. This is a sacred space, and I am only there at the permission of the host. Yong observes that, ". . . there is not only a continued reversal of roles, such that hosts become guests and vice versa, but sometimes we play both roles simultaneously."[57]

Credentialing, Certificates, and Licensure

Credentialing as a value was addressed on page 15. A related issue in professional chaplaincy is the question of licensing. The idea that chaplains should be licensed has been discussed among American chaplains for a number of years. While I agree with the principle, from a practical and pragmatic perspective, I believe the risks of pushing for chaplaincy licensure outweigh the benefits. The risk is that, in the current cultural and political climate in the United States, chaplains would lose whatever amount of control they now have over the standards for professional chaplaincy.

Writing in 2009 about hospital chaplains, Melvin Ray proposed an idealistic model, arguing that:

*No amount of organizing, education, and advo-
cacy will ensure the place of the professional
healthcare chaplain among the hospital team
until there is parity in formal standing and strict
accountability as with all other disciplines. A
bright line of demarcation must be established if
chaplaincy is to be recognized as a qualified,
clinical healthcare practice—legally accountable—and recognized as a healthcare profession
in all nuances of meaning. I would see this to be
accomplished when... state boards of chaplaincy are in place...* [58]

Wendy Cadge picked this up in 2012, writing,

*Rather than continuing to lobby the Joint Com-
mission to require hospitals to have chaplains,
as they have unsuccessfully for years, chaplaincy leaders might consider whether the time has
come for professional licenses like those required in medicine and nursing...*

*While the politics of licensing chaplains as re-
ligious or spiritual workers may be complex,
chaplains might at least want to consider
whether such efforts could help them regulate
the hiring of chaplains by hospitals, how they
are trained, and how they provide care. Licens-*

> *ing chaplains might help the profession to regulate not only the hiring of chaplains but the quality of care they provide.*[59]

While I agree with the idea of regulating the standards for professional chaplains, I do not think licensure is the way to achieve that goal. States grant licenses, and there would not be agreement on the requirements for being granted such a license. Professional chaplaincy would not be well served by having fifty different state licensing standards. One nationally recognized credential is preferable. With all due respect to elected and appointed government officials, any effort to license chaplains would result in the politicization of professional chaplaincy, and the handing over of authority to certify chaplains to people who lack the capacity to make that determination. My fear is that the standards would be much lower and professional chaplaincy as we know it would be undermined.

Historian Daniel Immerwahr observes that, "Standards reflect power, but the real compulsion rarely comes from the state. It comes, rather, from the community."[60] This dynamic is happening with credentialing of hospital chaplains. When enough institutions in a given market state a preference for board-certified chaplains and a critical mass has been reached, "that choice becomes practically mandatory."[61]

We are not there yet with EMS chaplaincy, though the Spiritual Care Association has worked to standardize the training and offers a Crisis, Trauma, and First Response Certificate, with clearly stated learning outcomes.[62] Another option for any agency considering hiring a chaplain is to inquire as to the credentialing expectations for hospitals in the region, and to consider adopting that standard as a requirement for their organization. This gives the chaplain options for supplemental employment, as well as networking with peers.

Lift Up:
Listening, Encouraging, Affirming

Enhancing Well-Being, Engagement, and Patient Care with Weak Ties

Approaching casual relationships intentionally in EMS has lasting implications for improving engagement and optimism in the EMS workforce. Think about a paramedic's typical workday, apart from the clinical aspects. Our medic gets to the base, where she sees a coworker, and asks about their weekend. Crews are coming and going; they chat for a few minutes and wish each other well. Our medic has a brief exchange with a supervisor or support staff person. Heading out, she makes her regular stop for coffee and a snack at the convenience store and shoots the breeze with the clerk. She then responds to a call, exchanging greetings with the police officers, and the fire and rescue team on scene. She may not know any of these people well, but their paths cross occasionally, and they engage in some light conversation.

It appears that these "weak ties" have a greater impact on our well-being than we realize.[63, 64] A 2014 study found that, "Daily interactions with casual acquaintances... can contribute to day-to-day well-being."[65]

Tracking interactions with family and friends (strong ties) and with acquaintances (weak ties), participants in the research reported a greater sense of belonging and happiness on the days when they had more weak-tie conversations. "Evidence suggests that weak ties such as these—relationships involving less frequent contact, low emotional intensity, and limited intimacy—confer some important benefits," the authors noted. The topic of weak ties moved into the public consciousness during the pandemic. As the coronavirus changes our routines to interact with fewer people on a daily basis, we shrink our network of important weak-tie relationships.[66]

Social relationships, with weak ties or strong ties, are an essential part of being human. Our brains are hard-wired to seek connection with other people. It's in all of our best interests to cultivate the fine art of making small talk with people we don't know very well.

Patient Care Implications

For EMS providers, this has implications for both their personal relationships and patient care. First, weak ties with those the providers encounter throughout the day benefit their own sense of well-being. Having casual contact with peers, public safety colleagues, hospital staff, and others deepens their sense of connectedness. In their article, "Mistakenly Seeking Solitude," Nicholas Epley and Juliana Schroeder report that, "Feeling socially connected increases happiness and health, whereas feeling disconnected is depressing and unhealthy."[67] Small talk aids in our ability to see others as fellow human beings, beyond the uniform.

Writing in *The New York Times*, Allie Volpe observes that, "Instead of considering these minor

brushes of socialization throwaway interactions, cultivating low-stakes relationships can pay dividends."[68]
Our intentional effort to nurture weak ties with those
around us also extends to patients. Making small talk
with patients and their loved ones invites providers to
look beyond the illness, beyond the circumstances that
bring EMS to their aid, and see them as fellow human
beings. The same benefits of social connection that we
enjoy—an increase in our happiness and health—also
benefit the patient.

Encouraging Empathy and Engagement

The practice of cultivating weak ties has potential
leadership, business, and institutional implications as
well. Writing in *The Wall Street Journal,* Jennifer
Breheny Wallace notes, "Chitchat is also an important
social lubricant, helping to build empathy and a sense
of community. It is much harder to snap at a [cowork-
er]… if you have just exchanged pleasantries."[69]

One of the tasks of the workplace chaplain is to
embody that "weak-tie" relationship. Likewise, I believe that managers who have an intentional, weak-tie
relationship with their direct reports are more likely to
have employees who are more engaged, resulting in
lower rates of employee turnover. Those employees
are also more likely to be more empathetic toward

their patients, which leads to increased patient satisfaction. Weak ties can be nurtured by the occasional social event, manager-provided food, and EMS Week activities. Work relationships have some natural boundaries, but that doesn't preclude being friendly and showing an interest in your employees.

It's clear that making small talk has surprising benefits. The challenge, and the opportunity, for EMS clinicians and leaders is to approach those interactions deliberately.

The time of a crisis is not the time for us to be shaking hands

---

Build Ties by Proactive Relationship Building and Outreach

One of the rules in EMS is that, except in specific situations, the paramedic or EMT does not self-deploy. They wait to be assigned to an incident and then respond. However, EMS chaplains act proactively as well as reactively. Chaplains take the initiative to build relationships with field providers, supervisors, and managers.

Being embedded with the workforce, the chaplain hears of high-stress incidents from a variety of sources. Local leadership and medical direction will determine whether a specific request or referral is in order prior to the chaplain's outreach after critical incidents. Working collaboratively with leadership, the first task is to acknowledge the situation and assess the need. If the person has adequate support, they may decline the offer of chaplaincy support. Every situation and every individual is different. My concern as chaplain is that they get support from *someone*. It may not be me, and that is OK.

Build Weak Ties by Assimilating into the Organization

Professional EMS chaplaincy involves learning and adapting to the culture of the organization. Chaplain Xolani Kacela's observations about military chaplaincy also apply to public safety chaplaincy: "You have to adapt quickly and find ways to assimilate or become a perpetual outsider. People who learn the culture and adapt to it will have a higher chance of success than those who resist assimilation and decide that they can change the culture."[70]

In the first few years after my position was created, the organization had no experience with a nonmedical professional routinely riding with ambulance crews and being present on scene. I was provided with a pair of navy blue standard-issue cargo pants and a dress shirt with "Chaplain" embroidered on the lapel.

Within a few months, one of the senior paramedics wrote to the chief, questioning whether I as the chaplain had earned the right to wear elements of the paramedic uniform. A colleague advised that it would not be in my best interests to engage in a debate with him, as I might be viewed as a "medic wannabe." I put the pants in my closet and wore navy blue dress pants during ride-alongs with crews, until several years later when the individual left the company.

By then I had a clearer sense of my own identity as an EMS chaplain. I also recognized that it was actually in my best interest—and in the interests of the company—if I had a uniform. Police and firefighters at the scene of an incident need to know at a glance who is present and their role in the response. Having a sweater with company patches on the shoulders, and a jacket with the word "Chaplain" across the back, makes it clear to everyone that I am part of the response team. In addition, my relationship with the ambulance crews and dispatchers has changed as I've become more embedded with the emergency responders.

Another way of assimilating is by the development of the chaplain's Standard Operating Procedures

(SOPs). Emergency Medical Services is an intensely protocol-driven industry, and the EMS chaplain is advised to learn the language. Creating SOPs for the chaplain's core activities and responsibilities will both standardize the chaplain's practice and communicate with the rest of the organization.

Chapter Four
"What"*

Putting It into Practice

Chapter Two introduced the value of operationalizing chaplaincy. This means applying the practices of business operations to the position—defining the scope of practice, creating SOPs, and defining the procedures for performance evaluation. These practices provide a level of transparency, showing that the chaplain is treated the same as other employees. Having these things documented also leaves a record for future chaplains coming into the organization, so they don't have to start over again, defining the position and its place in the organization.

The role of the chaplain to individuals is to provide professional, evidence-based chaplaincy support to frontline employees with the aim of mitigating the adverse effects of responding to critical incidents and accumulative stress. The chaplain is responsible for

---

*Strategy, consistent with "how"

serving the needs of frontline employees in the form of:

- Prevention (establishing a supportive relationship)
  - Ride- and sit-alongs with frontline staff
  - One-to-one time at the bases, by phone
  - Formal and informal education and social events
- Intervention (accompaniment or other active participation, referrals as needed)
  - During high-acuity critical incidents
  - During one-to-ones that result in the employee experiencing a mental health crisis or suicidal thoughts
- Postvention (listening, debriefing, following up)
  - One-to-ones and small groups, after specific high-acuity calls
  - With employees as follow-up after intervention

Private conversations with employees require strict boundaries, for the safety of everyone. (Note that it's common for conversations to heat up in the last fifteen minutes or so of the ride-along or meeting, so allow time for that.) In addition to field staff, the chaplain maintains professional and ongoing interpersonal relationships with organizational leaders. Support to leaders ranges from informal chats to formal interviews. Lunch and coffee are always good opportunities to connect.

Toleration of Pain in Self and Others

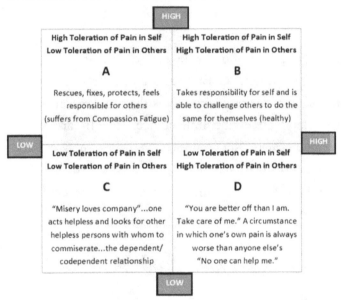

The role of the chaplain to the individual includes the relationship-building, informal interactions, and one-to-one follow-ups described previously. This work finds its focus in the awareness that EMS is a profession that carries a lot of emotional weight. Add to that the personality trait of many of us who work in trauma response to tolerate pain in ourselves more than others. The grid on the previous page illustrates the tension; while we may strive for quadrant B, we tend to be hard-wired for quadrant A.[71]

It has been my observation that many frontline EMS providers seem to cluster in quadrant A: willing to endure plenty of personal discomfort, but less willing to tolerate it in others. The benefit of this personality trait is that it makes us good clinicians. People with these characteristics excel at rescuing, fixing, and protecting. The downside is that we are at risk for compassion fatigue. Taking care of others comes naturally; taking care of ourselves does not. More will be said later about the importance of self-care for the chaplain; here, the point is to describe a common characteristic of the people in the care of the EMS chaplain, the world they live in, and the challenges they face.

Stresses of the EMS Provider

Of the seven stresses listed on the next page, much attention has been given to number 7, the critical incident, and for good reason. Many of us who work in this environment would agree and then add, "But this is what we do." We knew what we were getting into when we went into this field. The worst day of someone else's life is just another day at work for us.

1. Role expectations, performance, confidence
2. Operational workload, shiftwork, organization, management, and value proposition
3. Home/work interface
4. Social/political mismatch, loss of agency and control
5. Accumulated misery
6. Moral/spiritual injury
7. Overwhelming event or threat—the critical incident.

What we may not anticipate are the other six stresses. Cumulative stress and moral injury take their toll. One stressor, sometimes unexpected, is the job itself: the hours, the physical demands of not knowing when you might have time to use the restroom, working outside in all kinds of weather. These add to the weight of the job and merit acknowledgement and attention from the EMS chaplain. A friend, approaching his retirement after thirty-four years as a paramedic, spoke about the two goals he set for himself. One was to get into a regular routine of only sleeping at night.

Years of shift work had taken their toll. His second goal was to eat more slowly. Paramedics, EMTs, and dispatchers all live with the uncertainty of when the next call will come in, and the need to take advantage of any chance to grab a bite to eat. Post-EMS life would present the challenge and the opportunity to slow down, taking time to eat slowly.

Paramedics and EMTs who have worked both rural and urban areas observe that one of the stresses of working in a metro is the volume—more calls, with less downtime between calls. A common stress for rural EMS—especially those who live in the same rural and small-town communities where they work—is the increased possibility that they will be responding to calls for people they know. Working in rural EMS might mean recognizing the address before you leave the base. It may involve responding to calls for family, friends, and neighbors. Having a prior relationship with the patient can be an asset, and at the same time may make it difficult to keep an emotional distance while caring for a critically ill patient. The EMS chaplain is encouraged to be aware of this dynamic and acknowledge that a particular call may be difficult for a crew member providing care for someone they know from the community.

One of the stresses is the work/home interface. Being at work while your loved ones are at home can be a challenge. More than once I have been riding with ambulance crews when it gets to be the time of day when their families are having dinner. The phones come out, and a personal conversation begins. Those with young families may start a video chat with their children. If at all possible, I step outside and go for a short walk to give the paramedics and EMTs some privacy. We are whole people, and even though we may do our best to separate our work life from our home life, our loved ones are never too far outside our consciousness. Caring for our relationships is important and a sign of health. Those phone calls are a vital part of staying grounded.

Care of the Dispatchers

One group often overlooked for recognition and support are the dispatchers. Unlike the paramedics and EMTs who are highly visible in the community, dispatchers are rarely seen, though are actually the "first" first responders. They are exposed to the raw and unfiltered anguish of the caller, before anyone is on the scene. Dispatchers assess the situation, determine what resources are needed, give pre-arrival instructions, reassure the caller that help is on the way, and then end the call without learning of the outcome. At times there is little break between ending one call and answering the next. The chaplain is advised to be particularly attentive to the world of the emergency dispatcher.

Reaching Out, Offering Support

One of the hallmarks of EMS is our care and concern for each other. We have each other's backs. On a person-to-person, human level, we care. So, as far as the role of the person doing the outreach, it can be any of us—peer, supervisor, manager, friend. Rank and position are left at the door.

The goal of the outreach starts from the same place. Why do we reach out to someone who has had a tough call? Because we care. Because we know they would do the same for us. The goal is to let our colleagues know that we care. Not to fix them, not to take care of them, but simply to stand with them. Open the door.

The "how to" will depend on the relationship and how you usually communicate. Friends might make a phone call or send a text. Field supervisors might meet them at the hospital. Dispatch leaders might be immediately available in the same room.

In my case, I've found it most effective to start with a text message. I never know if someone might be available, working, or sleeping, so I hesitate to make phone calls. Plus, with text messages, I can send a brief message of support and leave it up to the recipient if or how they want to respond. A common text message that I use is: "Checking in with you after the (pediatric cardiac arrest) incident. Sounds like it had the potential to be stressful. I want you to know I'm aware of it and am available if I can be of support."

Responses vary. It may be that I don't hear anything in reply. Sometimes, it's a short, "Thanks, I'm doing OK but I really appreciate the outreach."

It may go like this: "I'm all right but am concerned about my partner. It seemed to hit him pretty hard." Occasionally, I get a long reply, detailing why the call was hard, putting it in the context of the medic's current situation, assuring me that they're OK. In effect, they are unloading the story, and the emotional weight that goes with it, in writing.

Sometimes, I get a text back: "That one was hard. I'd be interested in attending a CISD if one is held." That's a clue. I reply by offering to talk further—by phone, at a coffee shop, wherever and whenever they wish. One thing I've learned is not to send a text message stating that I'm available unless I truly am available, right then. It's happened where my text went out and within ten minutes the medic was calling my phone.

One of the simplest and most effective things

any of us can do to support our coworkers is to acknowledge their experiences. Don't assume that they're doing OK, traumatized, or anything in between. Sometimes, the best thing a supervisor can do is to take them out of service, even for a short time, without asking if they wanted it. "Take a half hour, get something to eat if you'd like." Asking crews if they want a break is a set-up. What are they supposed to say? "Yes, I'm traumatized," "No, I'm not," "Yes, I'd like a break, but I don't want my coworkers to have to take on extra work just so I can have a half hour to myself"?

Our first impulse may be to ask, "How are you?" but I've found it to be more helpful not to ask anything. Just tell them you're aware of the incident, express your concern and support, and keep your mouth shut. If they are visibly shaken, don't try to fix it. Everyone deserves the right to interpret their own experiences in their own way.

For one thing, they may not know how they're doing. They may be numb and not feeling much of anything. In the first hours after an incident, they're still loaded with the stuff our bodies give us to get through a crisis—adrenaline, cortisol, norepinephrine—and truly unable to feel anything.

So asking them how they're doing can be pointless, or even harmful, as it may lead to the impression that everything is fine. In fact, we often hear an initial response of "I'm fine" or "I'm OK." By waiting until the next day, after we've had some sleep, those chemicals have worn off and we're more aware of the emotional weight of the event.

Several days after one of our young paramedics responded to a suicide, he asked if we could meet at a coffee shop near the ambulance base. We exchanged some small talk as we got settled. When the conversation grew quiet, I asked about the call. At first it sounded like he was reciting his patient care report. Clinically, he and his partner had done everything they could. But there was something more. I asked, "What made this call critical for you?" Without hesitating, he replied softly, "He could have been one of my high school friends." *Yes*, I thought. *And when you're in your early twenties, high school wasn't that long ago.*

We sometimes tend to pathologize stress reactions, but we go into this business because we care about people, and coming face-to-face with human suffering does impact us. We don't want to be robots, and neither do the crews. We need to know that we're human, and sometimes that leads to tears. Stress is a normal response to an abnormal event.

So I try to start out that follow-up conversation with education, and the message that, "As hard as this is, it tells me that you're normal." Then I let them talk. They may recount the incident in detail. They may focus on the clinical aspects of the call and not go anywhere near the emotional impact. It doesn't matter. I've done my job.

The Role of the Chaplain in the Organization

Beyond supporting individuals in the EMS organization, the chaplain supports the organization itself, in both tangible and symbolic ways. Most common is through education related to well-being and self-care. Symbolically, the chaplain's presence at recognition ceremonies, social events, and being visible among employees signal that the company values and supports the workforce. Examples of the chaplain's role in supporting the organization include:

- Written communications (newsletters, social media posts)
- Contributing to employee education in ways that meet the organization's needs
- Sensitivity to the organization's cultural and spiritual/religious diversity. While respecting this diversity, the chaplain is creative and proactive in implementing rituals to

mark significant events in the life of the organization

One of the tasks of the EMS chaplain is to work collaboratively with the leadership team in identifying resources that will be needed in the event of a high-stress incident. This could involve development of a crisis response procedure to be implemented by the duty officer before the end of the shift; procedures and contact information for trained critical incident debriefers; mental health professionals experienced in trauma support; line-of-duty death procedures; and other resources that will be required on short notice.

In her book *First Responder Resilience: Caring for Public Servants*, psychologist Tania Glenn pointedly asks, "What's the plan?" Intentional, thoughtful planning is what makes possible the chaplain's work of prevention, intervention, and postvention. Building relationships with providers is essential if the chaplain is to respond on short notice. One of the resources that has met with mixed, and sometimes negative, reactions is the Employee Assistance Program. Glenn observes that, "The biggest mistake is to assume that just because clinicians are providers through your Employee Assistance Program (EAP), they are trained to understand what first responders do." She goes on to say that, "I cannot count the times leaders, first responders, and family members have told me the same horror stories about the EAP counselor whose jaw dropped during a session; [or] the EAP counselor who started to cry upon hearing the reason someone was seeking help…"[72]

This is not to paint all EAP programs with the same brush. The point is to learn the landscape, get to know the providers and their areas of expertise, and be prepared to help employees at those critical times to find the best resource. Chaplains and EMS leaders are encouraged to work with their EAP providers to identify mental health clinicians skilled in working with public safety providers whose everyday work exposes them to traumatic stress. EAP leaders are likewise encouraged to contract with vendors who can address the unique stressors facing EMS staff.

Measuring the Effectiveness of the Chaplain

The same as for every other employee, it is essential to have formal, well-designed evaluation tools for the EMS chaplain. This is another area in which the distinction between traditional and professional chaplaincy becomes clearer.[73] The traditional practice is largely subjective, assuming the inherent value of the institutional chaplain. Fairness and accountability require that the professional chaplain's work be gauged in much the same way as everyone else—by setting clear goals and expectations and measuring the chaplain's performance of those goals.

A common evaluation form gives the leader the option to rank the employee, along the lines of:

- Meets expectations
- Exceeds expectations
- Does not meet

When done well, this format will be based on specific annual goals, which will include both the on-going, core work that forms the basis of the position, as well as the occasional special project or initiative. These goals will be developed collaboratively by the chaplain and their manager, and reviewed and updated throughout the year as needs change. There are no surprises when it comes time for an annual review. Both parties will know whether the goals have been met. Below is an example of the kind of specific, measurable goals that a new EMS chaplain might set for their first year of service.

Sample Goals for a New EMS Chaplain
1. Engagement with frontline staff
   a. X number of ride-alongs/site visits

with ambulance crews
    b. X number of evening/weekend site visits/ride-alongs
    c. Timely follow-up with crews following critical incidents
2. Engagement with leaders
    a. X number of ride-alongs with supervisors
    b. One-to-one conversations with leaders
    c. Participation in leader meetings as appropriate
3. Engagement with the organization
    a. New employee/academy orientation to chaplain services
    b. Writing for newsletters, social media pages
    c. Participation in EMS Week, recognition programs, and other company-wide activities, and casual conversations with employees

In the case of things that are difficult to count or measure, there may be some other tool that leaders use to assess the performance of an employee. Here I'm thinking of a modified "360," where you might ask the people who work with the chaplain if they have any input or examples, illustrating the kind of work the person does. I do not support the use of Survey Monkey or other anonymous survey instruments, as they tend to bring out more negative than positive comments, which are not constructive. If someone has a legitimate concern about the chaplain's performance—or a compliment—that person can speak privately to the chaplain's manager or be willing to share their comments directly with the chaplain. The old adage, "What you permit, you promote" serves to caution leaders against allowing or inviting anonymous venting, which can be shaming to the recipient and toxic to the organization.

From my own experience, getting a routine evaluation or one obviously based on the evaluator's opinion is demoralizing and doesn't do much for my engagement with the organization. Earlier in my career I heard a manager say, "Well, it's been a good year, let's put you down for 'Exceeds,'" which told me they didn't put much time into my evaluation. A subjective evaluation is nice if the manager likes me, but why does it matter if my manager likes me? Below are two examples from the business community; these will be familiar to leaders who are accustomed to doing performance reviews for their other direct reports.

Locke and Latham offer five principles of effective goal setting:[74]

1. Clarity. A goal must be specific and clear.
2. Challenge. An easy or tedious goal is demotivating. But keep a realistic balance; don't expect anyone on your team to spin straw into gold.
3. Commitment. Your employees have to understand and buy in to the goal from the outset.
4. Feedback. Provide regular feedback throughout the whole process. This helps to keep the goal on track.
5. Task complexity. Think about realistic timescales and break down the process into subgoals with regular reviews.

SMART Goal Setting[75]

The method of SMART goals is one of the most effective tools used by high achievers to reach their goals consistently.

The SMART model of goal setting:

S = Specific

M = Measurable

A = Achievable

R = Relevant

T = Time-bound

Once your goals are SMART, break down each goal into specific, clear tasks and activities needed to accomplish the goal. It's important to periodically review your goals and make adjustments if necessary. Goal setting is an essential tool for success.

Self-Care

The Toleration of Pain grid on page 91 points to the need for EMS personnel to intentionally practice self-care. Self-care was one of the topics that led to the development of a proactive model of chaplaincy. I was familiar with the practice of critical incident debriefing, which usually includes some education about how to take care of oneself after a high-stress event. During the EMT course discussion of trauma, the instructor described the chain reaction of physical responses to stress that are set in motion. He was talking about the patient, but I realized that those are also the same things that happen to us as providers. This isn't new to paramedics, but it has some interesting implications for self-care.

The thyroid kicks in to regulate the speed of chemical reactions. Our metabolism is accelerated, burning fuel faster. Critical blood supplies are diverted to the heart, lungs, and muscles, carrying fuel and oxygen. Neurochemicals including adrenaline, cortisol, and norepinephrine are released into the blood-stream, giving us a burst of strength and energy to respond to the crisis. The blood diversion to the heart and lungs causes the digestive system to shut down. Since the stomach is shut down, the body goes into starvation mode, causing the body to crave carbohydrates.

What do we reach for in a crisis? Chips! Cookies! Fast food! A burger, fries, and soft drink give us the things our bodies crave, which I have come to describe as the "four food groups of a high stress day": sugar, salt, fat, and caffeine. Self-care and a focus on wellness lead us to think about how these foods will make us feel. One of our goals after a traumatic call is to return to our own baseline as soon as possible, with no sugar high or caffeine-induced jitters. Carbs and sugar cause the blood sugar to spike then fall, leading to exhaustion.

To recover from a high-stress event, healthy self-care practices tell us instead to eat a low-carb/high-protein diet, whole grains that digest slowly, and green leafy vegetables. Avoid alcohol, high-sugar soft drinks and fruit juices, and caffeine. Try to rest, even if you don't sleep. After a critical incident, a colleague observed, our blood is like a toxic sludge. To release the neurochemicals from our bloodstream, she said, we can "sweat it out, cry it out, or pee it out."

Exercise until you sweat. Let yourself cry. If neither of those are available options, drink a lot of water.

Self-Care and the EMS Chaplain

Self-care is also essential for the EMS chaplain. By virtue of doing their job of listening and supporting frontline staff, the chaplain is affected by the emotional weight of accompanying others. On days when I am not riding with a crew or sitting with a dispatcher, I sometimes hang around in the break room or lounge area at a base, striking up a conversation with anyone who happens by. A reliable conversation starter is to inquire about the impact of the job on one's home life, and the impact of one's home life on the job. This opens the door to deeper topics, deeper listening, and deeper connections. It is all part of the work of the EMS chaplain, and it can be exhausting. Those observing this activity may not recognize it as work at all. However, after four or five hours of "small talk" with employees, I may be ready for a break. Self-care is in order, so I take a walk, get something to eat, or otherwise occupy myself with something less intense.

The activity that most of us recognize as "chaplain work" is the support offered to employees who have been involved in a high-stress or critical incident. Researchers use the terms *trauma exposure response, secondary traumatic stress, vicarious traumatization, empathic strain,* or *secondary trauma.* Laura van Dernoot Lipsky includes trauma exposure response under a larger rubric: *trauma stewardship,* which "refers to the entire conversation about how we come to do this work, how we are affected by it, and how we make sense of and learn from our experiences."[76]

The chaplain is not immune from the stresses that are inherent in EMS. Many of us are drawn to this work for the same reasons as the paramedics, EMTs, and dispatchers, which puts us at risk for the same things. It is incumbent on the chaplain themselves as well as the leadership team to note the chaplain's need for support. Mental health providers, psychologists, and providers in any related field need to pay attention to their own, albeit secondary, exposure to trauma. It is more than a cliché to say that every therapist needs a therapist, and every chaplain needs a chaplain.

The saying about the time of crisis not being the time to be exchanging business cards also applies to the chaplain. Getting to know the chaplains in the area—especially trauma hospital chaplains, law enforcement chaplains, and fire chaplains—is an investment in self-care. Law enforcement and fire chaplains can also be a resource for support of families and community members after a critical incident. Online chaplain peer support is a good resource, as is connection with the chaplain-certifying organization.

***

It was a particularly heavy weekend involving four critical calls. I was on the phone for hours over those few days, checking in and following up with crews who were on those calls, listening to their accounts of what they had experienced. Monday morning at the senior leadership team's weekly check in, we noted those four calls and the outstanding work done by dispatchers and field staff. I commented to the group, "This debriefer needs a debriefing." Apparently, I looked as tired as I felt. A half hour later, I got a phone call from the EAP manager. One of the operations leaders had asked her to call me, knowing that I would appreciate some support. That expression of support carried me through the next week, knowing that the organization had my back.

Around that time, I came up with an idea for a slogan for ambulance services. It would be "High Expectations. High Support." This is a rewarding and challenging job. We have high expectations, and we should. But we also continuously work to create and nurture an organizational culture of support. We have high expectations of our frontline staff, and they have high expectations of us as leaders. We trust them to do their best in some very traumatic and difficult situations, and we promise them that we will support them in any way we can.

One evening when my daughters were in high school, one of them brought home the movie *Cold Mountain.* The film is set during the American Civil War and tells the story of a soldier who was separated from his loved ones and spent most of the movie trying to get home. At the end they finally are reunited, only to be met with tragedy. I was not happy with the way the movie ended and said so. "What a lousy ending!" I said. "That was a great story and would have been a great movie without ending in tragedy."

My teenaged daughter replied, "That's the way life is, Dad. Sometimes things don't work out."

"Tell me about it," I said. "If I want to hear a story with a sad ending, all I have to do is go to work."

That exchange surprised me and was the beginning of a greater awareness of how my job impacts me. I don't like the way my heart starts pounding when watching a thriller or murder mystery. It's fine with me that some of the EMS crews watch action movies when posted at the ambulance base, but I don't care to join them. I'd rather read or go for a walk.

My self-care preferences tend toward the tangible. Unlike other vocations and professions where people can step back and see, hear, touch, taste, and smell their work, emergency medical care providers have very little in the way of tangible evidence that we did anything. Some great stories, some run reports. We will not get tangible rewards from our jobs. So we must go out and create those experiences for ourselves. It can be anything creative or artistic. I like to engage with staff about what they like to do when they're not at work, listening to their descriptions of tapping maple trees and making maple syrup, pounding on metal in their garage blacksmith shop, competitive ballroom dancing, painting, photography, gardening, and myriad other things people do to keep their lives in balance.

This kind of mutual accountability contributes to the health and well-being of the entire workforce. Making self-care the norm is good for the mental health of all of us. This is not an expense, it's an investment. Our employees, their families, our communities, and our patients are all the recipients of this focus on the women and men who are out there every day. The EMS chaplain has an important role to play in the life and health of the organization. We are all the beneficiaries of this culture of support.

Flexibility and Creativity

A hallmark of workplace chaplaincy is the need for flexibility and creativity—being attentive to the needs of the organization and proactively addressing those needs. The pandemic of 2020–2021 has brought this need for flexibility into sharp focus. Even in the world of EMS, where "business as usual" is very broad, the coronavirus caused us to push harder to find ways to stay connected to the staff. We had to find ways to interact with field staff that didn't involve going on calls. Having a rider in the confined space of an ambulance was not in the best interests of the health and safety of the crews, patients, or chaplains. We had to innovate. Like chaplains in other settings, we found different ways to connect, including Facebook Live, Zoom, and other electronic media.

However, electronic communications have their limits, because, as Geoff Colvin writes in *Fortune* magazine, "We are hardwired to value the physical presence of others… Shaking hands is literally an electric experience: Brain imaging shows that we energize the region associated with reward sensitivity—that is, we feel rewarded—by shaking hands or merely seeing other people shake. There is a similar physical response when we converse with someone face-to-face. The pupils of our eyes constrict and dilate in parallel with the other person's. Neither of us is aware it's happening, but it builds trust."[77]

While we weren't going on calls with ambulance crews, we continued to have in-person interactions at the bases (wearing masks and six feet apart). Showing up at shift change time with a plate of cookies is always a good way to start a conversation, too.

Any time, under any conditions, the chaplain starts by listening. EMS personnel tend to be wired to assess and solve problems. People usually have or find resources to deal with their losses, be it a difficult call, death of a loved one, working during a pandemic, or other life challenges. So while they're not looking to their employer to take care of them, they deeply appreciate the outreach. An honest expression of concern and a willingness to listen are the strongest message you can give. The message that speaks loudest is, "You're not alone or forgotten. You are important. You are valued. I'm thinking of you."

Acknowledgements

I am indebted to many people for the completion of this book. My sincere thanks to:

The paramedics, EMTs, dispatchers, and van drivers of Allina Health EMS, for allowing me to accompany you. You do some amazing work under challenging conditions every day; the world is a better place because of you.

The Allina EMS leadership, clinical services, and support teams: your trust and support make this work possible.

Brian LaCroix, for your vision and your trust.

Lori Boland, epidemiologist and researcher: the well-being studies would not have happened without your guidance and leadership.

The community of chaplains: you get it in ways that few others do.

The students, staff, and faculty at United Theological Seminary: keep pushing the boundaries and asking the hard questions.

All of you who read and commented on early drafts of the book.

EMS1: several sections of this book were first published on EMS1.com. Those sections are reprinted with permission.

King Features, for permission to reprint the cartoon on page 43.

My wife, Mary: thanks for your partnership and support.

Lastly, to Daniel: hanging out with a nine-year-old is good for my soul and reminds me of what is truly important. I can change out of my uniform and just be Grandpa. I'll always have time for a game of tag.

About the Author

Russell Myers serves as a chaplain for Allina Health Emergency Medical Services, based in Minneapolis. He holds a BA from Ohio State University and a Doctor of Ministry degree from Luther Seminary, St. Paul, Minnesota. Russ is ordained by the Evangelical Lutheran Church in America and is board certified with the Association of Professional Chaplains.

He lives in Saint Paul, Minnesota. You can contact Russ at russellnmyers@yahoo.com.

Notes

Preface

[1] Modeled after Wolf, Maryanne. *Proust and the Squid*. New York: HarperCollins, 2007

[2] Sinek, Simon. *Start with Why: How Great Leaders Inspire Everyone to Take Action*. New York: Penguin, 2009

Chapter One

[3] CPE is offered by these and other training centers: Association for Clinical Pastoral Education (www.acpe.edu) , Canadian Association for Spiritual Care (www.spiritualcare.ca), Institute for Clinical Pastoral Training (www.icpt.edu), Spiritual Care Association (www.spiritualcareassociation.org/cpe-org)

[4] Clouzet, Lisa. "Chaplaincy: Are you called?" Ministry International Journal for Pastors, July 2018 https://www.ministrymagazine.org/archive/2018/07/Chaplaincy-Are-you-called (accessed 9/29/2020)

[5] Val Ulstad, personal correspondence, 2012

[6] Heath, Chip and Dan Heath. *Decisive: How to make better choices in life and work.* 2013, New York: Crown Business. Pages 135ff

[7] See Workplace Chaplaincy, Princeton University Faith & Work Initiative (https://faithandwork.princeton.edu/research/workplace-chaplaincy)

[8] Stewart-Darling, Fiona. *Multifaith Chaplaincy in the Workplace: How Chaplains can Support Organizations and their Employees.* London: Jessica Kingsley, 2017. Page 17

[9] Ibid., pages 40-41

[10] Psychological First Aid (PFA) is an evidence-informed approach that is built on the concept of human resilience. PFA aims to reduce stress symptoms and assist in a healthy recovery following a traumatic event, natural disaster, public health emergency, or even a personal crisis. (see https://www.ptsd.va.gov/professional/treat/type/psych_firstaid_manual.asp)

[11] Critical incident debriefing is a formal process in which those involved in a traumatic event can talk with others who were also present, usually within three days of the event. (see www.icisf.org)

[12] Patterson, P. Daniel, et al. "The Longitudinal Study of Turnover and the Cost of Turnover in Emergency Medical Services" in Prehospital Emergency Care, April/June 2010, Vol. 14, No. 2 https://www.tandfonline.com/doi/abs/10.3109/10903120903564514

[13] Paget, Naomi K. and Janet R. McCormack. *The Work of the Chaplain.* 2006, Valley Forge, PA: Judson Press

[14] Immerwahr, Daniel. *How to Hide an Empire: a History of the Greater United States.* 2019, New York: Farrar, Straus and Giroux, page 299

[15] https://www.nremt.org/rwd/public

[16] See note 10

[17] Ordination is a process by which individuals in religious or faith communities are authorized to perform religious ceremonies. A person who gains this official status in their religious community is *ordained*

[18] Clouzet

[19] Cobb, M., C. Swift and A. Todd, "Introduction to Chaplaincy Studies," 2015. In *A Handbook of Chaplaincy Studies: Understanding Spiritual Care in Public Places.* Swift, Cobb and Todd, eds. (page 2) Surrey, England: Ashgate

[20] Cobb, Swift and Todd, p. 4

[21] Ibid, p. 3

[22] Cadge, Wendy. *Paging God: Religion in the Halls of Medicine.* 2012. Chicago: The University of Chicago Press.

[23] https://www.spiritualcareassociation.org/crisis-trauma-and-first-response-certificate-course-for-chaplains

https://www.spiritualcareassociation.org/first-responder-chaplains.html

[24] An internet search will provide a list of chaplaincy certifying organizations. The reader is encouraged to vet these organizations when deciding which credential to accept.

[25] Relating to or affecting the human spirit.

[26] Billings, Alan. "The Place of Chaplaincy in Public Life," 2015. In *A handbook of chaplaincy studies*. (p. 43)

[27] Gleason, John J. "Can Chaplains Survive and Thrive with P4P?" https://www.professionalchaplains.org/files/publications/chaplaincy_today_online/volume_28_number_2/28_2gleason.pdf accessed 11/18/2020

[28] Billings, p. 34

[29] Ibid, p. 35

[30] Ibid, p. 40

[31] Ibid, p. 40

[32] Ibid, p. 41

[33] This section draws on the work of Billings, Alan. "The Place of Chaplaincy in Public Life," 2015. In *A handbook of chaplaincy studies,* the subsection "Making the Case for Chaplaincy—Adding Value" *(pp. 41-42)*

[34] Patterson, ibid.

[35] Three-legged stool description modeled after Natapoff, Alexandra. *Punishment Without Crime*. 2018. New York: Basic Books

Chapter Two

[36] Sinek, page 84

[37] Sinek, pages 104-105

[38] Kuang, Cliff with Robert Fabricant. *User Friendly: How the Hidden Rules of Design are Changing the Way we Live, Work, and Play.* New York: Farrar, Straus and Giroux. 2019. Page 328

[39] An Institutional Review Board (IRB) is a type of committee that applies research ethics by reviewing the methods proposed for research involving human subjects, to ensure that they are ethical. Also known as an independent ethics committee (IEC), ethical review board (ERB), or research ethics board (REB). See also https://en.wikipedia.org/wiki/Institutional_review_boa rd

[40] Boland, Lori et al. "Burnout and Exposure to Critical Incidents in a Cohort of Emergency Medical Services Workers from Minnesota" *Western Journal of Emergency Medicine*, Vol. 19, Issue 6, 2018. https://escholarship.org/uc/item/1wn2k7ng

[41] Ibid.

[42] Jeruzal, Jessica et al "Emergency Medical Services Provider Perspectives on Pediatric Calls: A Qualitative Study" *Prehospital Emergency Care*, Vol. 23, Issue 4 2019 https://www.tandfonline.com/eprint/pBhwJkZ5KRnP 2NDjdHc6/full

Chapter Three

[43] Paget, N.K., and McCormack, J.R. (2006). *The Work of the Chaplain.* Valley Forge, PA: Judson Press, p. 27

[44] Lakoff, George and Mark Johnson. *Metaphors We Live By.* 1980. Chicago: University of Chicago Press

[45] Pattison, Stephen (2015), "Situating Chaplaincy in the United Kingdom: The Acceptable Face of 'Religion" In Swift, Christopher, Mark Cobb, and Andrew Todd, eds. *A handbook of chaplaincy studies: Understanding spiritual care in public places,* Surrey, England: Ashgate (pp. 23-24)

[46] Christian Bible, New Testament, Luke 10:30-35 *The Message* https://www.biblegateway.com

[47] Benemerito, Leah C. Unpublished paper, "Theological Foundations for Chaplaincy" used by permission and adapted for EMS by Russell Myers, April 17, 2015

[48] https://www.psychologytoday.com/us/blog/meaningful-you/201312/the-power-and-strength-bearing-witness Accessed 6/23/2018

[49] Jarvis, Kiersten. "Sherpa for the Soul," unpublished paper, 2016. Used by permission, 11/13/2020

[50] Hanson, Karen. "Accompaniment: Reflections from a Hospital Chaplain." *Bearings*, Spring 2014 https://collegevilleinstitute.org/wp-content/uploads/2013/02/Bearings6web.pdf Accessed 05/25/2018

[51] Mauldin, Jane Ellen, "Inherent Worth and Dignity" in *The Call to Care,* Hutt, Karen L., ed. Boston: Skinner House Books, 2017. Page 8

[52] Meskinoff, Nathan "Lost (and Found) in Translation" in *The Call to Care*, Karen L., ed. Boston: Skinner House Books, 2017. Pages 50-51

[53] Newell, J. Philip. *Listening for the Heartbeat of God: A Celtic Spirituality.* Mahwah, NJ: Paulist Press, 1997

[54] Ibid.

[55] www.bcci.professionalchaplains.org accessed 5/19/2018

[56] Sacks, Jonathan. The Chief Rabbi's New Year Message2001/5762 Given a few days after 9/11/2001 http://www.chiefrabbi.org/ReadArtical.aspx?id=359 accessed 5/3/2011

[57] Yong, Amos. *Hospitality and the other.* Maryknoll, New York: Orbis Books, 2008. Page 107

[58] Melvin Ray, "The Case For Chaplaincy Licensure," *Plain Views*, Vol. 6 No. 9, http://plainviews.healthcarechaplaincy.org/articles/The-Case-for-Chaplaincy-Licensure

[59] Cadge, ibid. pp. 206-207

[60] Immerwahr, page 328

[61] Ibid.

[62] https://www.spiritualcareassociation.org/crisis-trauma-and-first-response-certificate-course-for-chaplains

https://www.spiritualcareassociation.org/first-responder-chaplains.html

[63] Wallace, Jennifer Breheny. "The Benefits of a Little Small Talk" *The Wall Street Journal*, October 1, 2016 https://www.wsj.com/articles/the-benefits-of-a-little-small-talk-1475249737

[64] Volpe, Allie. "Why You Need a Network of Low-Stakes, Casual Friendships" *The New York Times*, May 6, 2019 https://www.nytimes.com/2019/05/06/smarter-living/why-you-need-a-network-of-low-stakes-casual-friendships.html accessed 11/11/2019

[65] Sandstrom, Gillian M. and Elizabeth W. Dunn. "Social Interactions and Well-being: the surprising power of weak ties" *Personality and Social Psychology Bulletin*, April 25, 2014 https://journals.sagepub.com/doi/abs/10.1177/0146167214529799

[66] https://www.bbc.com/worklife/article/20200701-why-your-weak-tie-friendships-may-mean-more-than-you-think

[67] Epley, Nicholas and Juliana Schroeder. "Mistakenly Seeking Solitude." *Journal of Experimental Psychology*, 2014 https://psycnet.apa.org/record/2014-28833-001

[68] Volpe, ibid.

[69] Wallace, ibid.

[70] Kacela, Xolani. "Military Chaplaincy, A Natural Fit" in *The call to care,* Hutt, Karen L., ed. Boston: Skinner House Books, 2017. Page 135

Chapter Four

[71] From the workbook "Leadership in Healthy Congregations," https://www.healthycongregations.com

[72] Glenn, Tania. *First Responder Resilience: Caring For Public Servants.* Aledo, Texas: Progressive Rising Phoenix Press, 2017

[73] Gleason, ibid.

[74] https://peakon.com/us/blog/future-work/edwin-locke-goal-setting-theory/ (accessed 11/02/2020)

[75] https://www.briantracy.com/blog/business-success/business-success-smart-goals-frugal-living/ (accessed 11/02/2020)

[76] van Dernoot Lipsky, Laura. *Trauma Stewardship: An Everyday Guide to Caring for Self While Caring for Others.* Oakland, CA: Berrett-Koehler Publishers, 2009. p. 6

[77] Colvin, Geoff. "Losing Connection," *Fortune*, August/September 2020, p. 21

Gryphon's Key Publishing is an independent publisher. We offer wholesale discounts and multiple binding options with no minimum purchases. Please visit our website to see our updated list of titles:

www.GryphonsKeyPublishing.com

and who will be categorized as the unacceptable Other. The pairing of the Rahab and Achan episodes back-to-back in chs. 6 and 7 undermines the initial impression, given by the battle sequences in the text, that ethnicity is paramount. The two stories illustrate the process of negotiations and exchanges by which insiders may become outsiders and outsiders may become insiders. Comparison of Rahab's behavior and fate with Achan's reveals that the true organizing principle of the narrative is not ethnic identity, but voluntary submission to authority structures, including the patriarchal political arrangement as well as the central ruling establishment represented by Joshua. The usual punishment for Otherness is death and destruction, as demonstrated by the many incidents in which all the Canaanites of a city or territory were 'slain with a great slaughter' or 'struck with the edge of the sword', leaving 'no survivor'. Yet the Canaanite Rahab is spared, along with everyone and everything under her (possessions and relatives), while Achan, along with his possessions and relatives, is violently destroyed. Although Rahab is a woman, she is described as a head of household in patriarchal language, almost as though she were a man:

> So the young men who were spies went in and brought out Rahab and her father and her mother and her brothers and all she had; they also brought out all her relatives and placed them outside the camp of Israel (Josh. 6.23).

While she remains in a transitional situation 'outside the camp of Israel', her femaleness is temporarily ignored in the text, and so is her low status as a prostitute; for once she is simply 'Rahab', rather than 'Rahab the harlot', her usual appellation. Then in v. 25 she is put into her hierarchical 'place' (in accordance with the patriarchal values of the text), with her father designated as head of the household, as she and her relatives settle permanently in the midst of Israel:

> However, Rahab the harlot and *her father's household* and all that she had, Joshua spared; and she has lived in the midst of Israel to this day (Josh. 6.25, [italics mine]).

Thus Rahab and her family were 'spared' the usual punishment for Otherness (death). The contrasting fate of the rest of the inhabitants of Jericho is graphically spelled out:

> And they (Joshua's men) utterly destroyed all in the city, both man and woman, young and old, and ox and sheep and donkey, with the edge of the sword (Josh. 6.21).

As in the battle reports of chs. 10 and 11 (cited earlier), the emphasis is on total destruction. By her voluntary submission to Joshua's authority and her acknowledgment of Yahweh (Josh. 2.11), Rahab was transformed from the quintessential Other into an insider deemed worthy of protection (and life). She accepted the structures of control and was allowed a place within the hierarchy of insiders. Achan, on the other hand, forfeited his place within the hierarchical system, although he was a born insider, by his attempt to circumvent the structures of control. His lack of submission to the lines of authority placed him (along with his offspring, because of the patriarchal nature of the system) outside the boundaries of control, thereby earning him (and them) the standard punishment for Otherness: a violent death.

The primary ideological purpose of the conquest narrative is to send a message to internal rivals, potential Achans, that they can make themselves into outsiders very easily. The text is more concerned with demonstrating to the internal populace the extent of the governing authorities' strength than with sending to external groups (real ethnic 'Others') a statement about their military capabilities. The in-group, headed by King Josiah, was motivated by the need to constitute itself as a power structure in the wake of imperial domination.

INDEXES

INDEX OF REFERENCES

OLD TESTAMENT

INDEX OF AUTHORS

THE BIBLICAL SEMINAR

JOURNAL FOR THE STUDY OF THE OLD TESTAMENT
SUPPLEMENT SERIES